Better Assessment in Higher Education

Better Assessment in Higher Education

A Universal Design for Learning Approach

KEVIN L. MERRY

UNTIL LEARNING HAS NO LIMITS™

Bulk discounts available: For details, email publishing@cast.org or visit www.castpublishing.org

Copyright © 2025 by CAST, Inc.
All rights reserved.

No part of this publication may be reproduced or transmitted in any form or by any means, electronic or mechanical, including photocopy, recording, or any information storage and retrieval systems, without permission in writing from the publisher.

Library of Congress Control Number: 2025934680

Paperback ISBN 978-1-943085-35-4
Ebook ISBN 978-1-943085-36-1

Published by:
CAST Professional Publishing
an imprint of CAST, Inc.
Lynnfield, Massachusetts, USA

SKINNY BOOKS® is a registered trademark of CAST, Inc.

Cover and interior design by Happenstance Type-O-Rama
Cover illustration: © Getty Images | fonikum

Contents

About the Author vii

Preface ix

PART I: Key Concepts: Setting the Scene

1 What Is Assessment and Why Do We Do It? . . . 3

2 Assessment and Intentional Learning Design . . 9

3 Assessment as a Support for
Expert Learning 15

4 Assessment and the UDL Principles 21

5 Holistic Assessment Considerations 29

PART II: Assessment Design

6 Learning Outcomes and Assessment 39

7 Assessment Barriers 47

8 Assessing Knowledge and Skills 57

9 Evaluating Your Assessments 63

PART III: Putting It All Together

10 Bringing Assessment Into the Classroom . . . 71

11 Diagnostic Assessment 79

12 Assessment for Metacognitive Development 85

13 Cheat-Proof Assessment 93

Epilogue 103

References and Further Reading 105

About the Author

Kevin L. Merry is an expert in accessible, inclusive, and equitable instructional design. He has supported the adoption and application of Universal Design for Learning (UDL) at educational institutions, including schools and school improvement programs in Europe, North America, and Asia. Kevin supports curriculum and instructional design, provides professional development and training, and develops resources and materials to support UDL implementation, helping educators to meet learners where they are right now, and showing how, when designed in the right way, learning can truly have no limits. An award-winning teacher, Kevin has received accolades for his approaches to accessible and inclusive curriculum design, and has become internationally renowned for his work on UDL. Kevin is founder and chair of the UDL United Kingdom and Ireland Education Network (UDL-UKI), the purpose of which is to identify, promote, and support the development of approaches, models, tools, and practices that enable effective UDL implementation in all education settings.

Preface

This book is an introduction to assessing student learning from a Universal Design for Learning (UDL) perspective in higher education contexts. It is intended primarily for those teaching in higher education, though it will be useful to anyone with an interest in learning, teaching, and, particularly, assessment in educational settings.

The book is split into three parts. Part I introduces the purposes of assessment, explores how assessment can support learning as part of intentional learning design, and discusses assessment's place within a UDL-centered approach to supporting learning. Part II gives detailed guidance on how to take a UDL-oriented approach to assessment design, outlining important considerations relating to authenticity and validity, as well as approaches to evaluating the accessibility, inclusivity, and equitability of assessment designs. Part III is about integrating all the advice from Parts I and II and explores how assessment can become part of the instructional experience for a multitude of purposes, including effective differentiated instruction and the development of learner metacognition. Part III also discusses how effective assessment designs can discourage learners from engaging in various forms of cheating and academic misconduct.

Part I

Key Concepts: Setting the Scene

1

What Is Assessment and Why Do We Do It?

The What of Assessment

In the most basic sense, assessment is the means by which teachers intentionally and methodically collect, interpret, and use information about how well their learners understand a given topic or concept in order to make educational decisions (Meyer et al., 2014; Salvia et al., 2009). "Understand" in this sense may refer to what the learners know about the topic, and it may also include their skills and abilities in relation to that topic or, put more plainly, what they're able to "do" as a result of their learning. Learning represents a personal and essential process of *meaning making* in the brain of the learner, based on their experience and prior learning and, of course, on what they learn through instruction (Petty, 2014). Meaning making is a physical process in the sense that learning is encoded in the brain as a network of neural connections (Petty, 2014). Of course, we are unable to look into our learners' brains at their neural connections to check that they have learned effectively, so we have to do it in an indirect way—and this is where assessment comes in.

Because we cannot directly evaluate our learners' neural connections, all learning assessment is essentially an approximation of the learning that has taken place. Hopefully, by remembering this critical limitation, we can commit more fully to selecting the most appropriate and effective assessments for a given learning situation, and that is what this book is about; we can also be more mindful of the fact that if we design assessments with inherent barriers, this limitation will be even more pronounced. Hence, by focusing on reducing and/or removing barriers, UDL strives to enable the most accurate approximation possible of learning through assessment.

As well as giving us an idea of how well learners understand a topic or how well they are able to do something as a result of their learning, assessment is also a critical mechanism for providing feedback on our teaching. For example, learner performance in various assessment tasks—in terms of both the processes they apply to such tasks as well as the products of those tasks—provides important information that we can use to adjust our teaching strategies or approaches (Rose et al., 2008; Rose et al., 2018). Unfortunately, we are not very good at using assessment for this purpose in higher education, and thus we miss out on a great opportunity to teach more effectively. Effective UDL practitioners are committed to continually improving their practice as a means of supporting learners based on where they are right now. Using assessment as a mechanism for feedback on teaching, alongside other important evaluation strategies, is a critical part of developing the iterative enhancements characteristic of effective UDL implementation.

The Why of Assessment

The broad purpose of assessment in higher education is multifaceted. For example, Archer (2017) introduced the *assessment purpose triangle*, a useful way of summarizing the three main purposes of assessment in education contexts, including higher education: assessment for accountability; assessment for certification, progress, and transfer; and assessment to support learning. Figure 1 shows a simplified version of the triangle.

The three purposes can be described as follows:

Accountability

This side of the triangle represents the responsibility educational institutions have to the public and/or government to provide evidence that learning is being promoted and subsequent academic standards are being upheld (Archer, 2017). Institutions often achieve this by comparing their learner results to various benchmarks

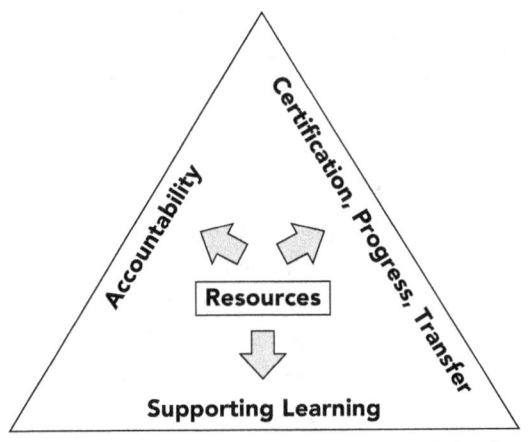

FIGURE 1: A simplified assessment purposes triangle (Archer, 2017)

for the sector or an applicable group (Archer, 2017). Since UDL is about removing or reducing barriers to enable learners to demonstrate learning most effectively, it can play an important strategic role in the assessment accountability agenda for universities to establish that learning is being promoted.

Certification, progress, and transfer

Certification, progress, and transfer is often associated with *assessment of learning*, also known as *summative assessment*. This side of the triangle can operate at both individual and institutional levels. For example, programs of learning frequently are required to be accredited by an accrediting body to support further study and potential employment (Archer, 2017). Hence, at the institutional level, accreditation provides verification that the program meets the standards and requirements set by the accrediting body. At the individual level, accreditation endorses the requirement for individual learners to attain particular knowledge, skills, and abilities. Once they've done so and achieved certification, learners may progress to the next level of learning or even transfer to a different institution (Archer, 2017).

Supporting learning

Assessment to support learning is effectively assessment *for* learning, also known as *formative assessment* (Archer, 2017), but may also include assessment *as* learning, which involves learner self-assessment and reflection. Assessment *for* and assessment *as* learning may both be used diagnostically to help identify learning strengths, pinpoint areas for learning development, and gauge learning progress. Both can also help inform learners and teachers of the extent to which learning has occurred at the time of assessment as well as how much subsequent learning is required before mastery is attained (Black et al., 2010). As a result of these assessments, learners may modify their approaches to learning and study, and—since both types can also be used to probe learner responses to instruction—teachers may modify their instruction (Rose et al., 2008; Rose et al., 2018). Differentiated instruction and, in particular, feedback often result from assessment *of* learning approaches, which can be integrated into the instructional experience or applied as discrete activities. UDL is about supporting learners to become expert learners by mastering the content of their learning and to gain an awareness of how they do so. Assessment *for* and assessment *as* learning are central ingredients to becoming an expert learner, demonstrating UDL's relevance to this core assessment purpose.

PAUSE AND THINK

- Do you currently use learner performance in assessment tasks as a mechanism for evaluating your teaching? If not, can you start doing so?

- To what extent are your current assessment processes supporting learning?

2

Assessment and Intentional Learning Design

Assessment is a critical feature of intentional learning design. When we are designing any learning experience, the intentional learning design model (Meyer et al., 2014) provides a useful "blueprint" to follow. The model, shown in Figure 2, consists of four parts in the following order:

1. Learning goals or outcomes
2. Assessments
3. Methods
4. Materials

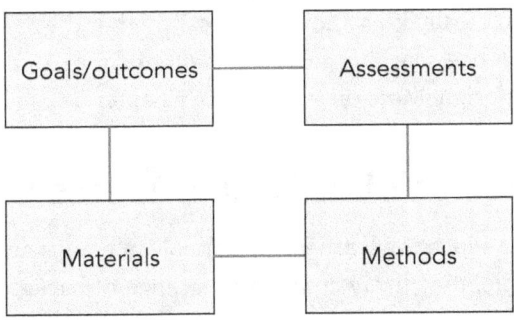

FIGURE 2: The intentional learning design model (Meyer et al., 2014)

The order of the model used to be goals/outcomes, methods, materials, and assessment. Placing assessments as the final element of the model generated the unhelpful idea that assessments are a less integrated part of instructional methods and materials, and generally reflect only summative assessment conventions. The modified order represents the refreshed emphasis on assessment as an integrated part of instruction (Meyer et al., 2014).

Goals or outcomes tend to be fixed, whereas the other three parts of the model are more flexible. It can be useful to think of the goals or outcomes as the "destination" of learning, with the other three parts of the model as the "journey" to that destination. Where we're going might be fixed, but how we get there—including assessment—is not; indeed, a key UDL principle is that assessments are flexible (Meyer et al., 2014).

The intentional learning design model reminds us of the importance of backward design (Wiggins & McTighe, 2005). In backward design, we first define the outcomes or goals, stating what we want our learners to know or be able to do. We then work out how we can assess what we want our learners to know or do. Following that, we work out a "pathway" that supports achievement of the learning outcomes or goals, including the assessment. Without knowing what the learning goals or outcomes are, then, we can't really know how to assess whether they've been met. Hence, learning goals are the foundation of assessment design. More on this topic in Chapter 6.

Fixed Goals but Flexible Assessments

Higher education learners are variable in many ways. For example, they likely come from a range of backgrounds and differ by age, ethnicity, gender, disability, sexual orientation, social class, and faith, among other factors. It is also likely they will arrive in higher education with a multitude of experiences and learning needs, a mix of emotional needs, and varying levels of motivation for and confidence with learning. As a result, learners will differ in how they approach and engage with the higher education learning environment, including the way in which they demonstrate their learning (assessment).

In response to learner variability, we must design assessments such that they enable all learners to demonstrate their learning in an effective way. The design should focus on reducing or removing barriers that might prevent a learner from effectively demonstrating their understanding. For example, requiring learners to handwrite their answers to an exam question (as has long been common practice in higher education) could present a barrier for any learner with dysgraphia, dyspraxia, dyslexia, or poor handwriting.

If the exam is administered under strictly timed conditions (as most exams are), it presents a further barrier for anyone that handwrites slowly. A common workaround has been to allow learners with declared disabilities or learning differences "reasonable adjustments" to complete their exams, such as the use of a word processor and extra time. However, the learner with poor handwriting who writes slowly would not usually have access to these accommodations. Neither would the international learner whose first language is not English and who subsequently reads and writes slowly in English.

Hence, rather than provide individual adjustments for specific learners to alleviate their challenges, it is better to examine the wider environment for barriers and work to reduce or remove them, remembering that barriers are always environmental, never within the learner. For example, removing restrictive time constraints in exams enables all learners to calmly plan and compose their answers. Allowing all learners to word-process their answers means nobody has to worry about whether their writing is legible.

If the exam is "unseen" (meaning the questions are not made available to learners before the exam) and "closed book" (meaning that learners are unable to use resources such as notes, glossaries, or textbooks during the exam), then learners with working memory and organizational challenges, such as those with attention deficit disorder (ADD), may be placed at a substantial disadvantage.

However, all learners can benefit from knowing what the questions are, which supports them in planning their answers, and from using supporting materials to help them rather than having to recall everything from memory.

This example is for illustrative purposes only and does not represent all accessibility, inclusivity, and equitability concerns or indeed effective assessment design considerations that we might want to account for. We do not know the purpose of the example assessment or what is actually being assessed, which would naturally influence our selection of assessment methods. For example, contextual authenticity and occupational relevance would be important considerations for selecting the appropriate assessment method. More on this subject in Chapter 8.

However, irrespective of what the exam intends to assess, we can easily see that it is also assessing a bunch of other factors—handwriting, time management, memory, and organizational skill, to name just a few. These irrelevant constructs effectively represent barriers, as Chapter 7 will discuss in more depth.

PAUSE AND THINK

- Are your current teaching methods, materials, and assessment methods flexible?

- Think about one of your current assessments. Can you identify any barriers that may prevent learners from clearly demonstrating their learning?

3

Assessment as a Support for Expert Learning

The key purpose of UDL is to support learners to become *expert learners*. An expert learner can be defined by two important characteristics (summarized in Figure 3): the ability to master the content of their learning by applying a range of cognitive and practical skills, and an awareness of their personal approach to achieving this mastery. Thus, there's an important metacognitive element to becoming an expert learner; becoming aware of one's personal approach to mastering the content of learning is effectively *learning how to learn*.

```
        Supporting learners to
        become "expert learners"
          /                \
Achieving mastery of    Knowing how to master
  learning content        learning content
```

FIGURE 3: What it means to be an expert learner

These two key characteristics of the expert learner are intimately bound with the assessment process. Indeed, both characteristics require assessment in order to be fulfilled. For example, the main way in which we determine whether a learner has mastered the content of their learning is through summative assessment techniques. Summative assessment, sometimes called assessment of learning, is perhaps the most common form of assessment. By having a learner complete various performance tasks, it aims to assess the extent to which the learner understands the information, ideas, concepts, and skills taught during a unit of study. Grades are usually awarded following summative assessment tasks, and the learner is required to achieve some threshold score in order to "pass" the assessment.

Summative assessments determine the outcomes learners achieve for the units and programs they study. For example, most higher education program grades are derived from the average grade achieved across the units or courses that compose those programs. For this reason, summative assessments are typically "high stakes," meaning there are potential consequences for performing poorly, such as failing to reach the passing grade (that is, the learner effectively fails the assessment) or failing to achieve the grade needed to maintain the desired overall grade average. For example, a learner may require a grade at or above 70% in an individual assessment in order to maintain a grade average at or above 70%. However, if the learner only achieved, say, 50% in their assessment, this would likely pull their average grade down to below 70%. Summative assessment is frequently the mechanism through which the certification, progress, and transfer (Archer, 2017) purpose of assessment, introduced in

Chapter 1, is fulfilled. Summative assessment design is covered in more detail in Chapters 6–8.

Developing a personal awareness of how to master the content of learning is more closely related to formative assessment. Sometimes called assessment for learning, formative assessment is intended to help teachers and learners gather evidence about where the learners are in relation to their learning and the direction and supports they need to achieve learning goals, providing continual feedback on strengths and areas for development (Gardner, 2011). As a monitoring tool for teachers and learners, it is intended to support learners with learning to learn. Typically, formative assessment does not involve grades but is instead centered on qualitative feedback. Formative assessment is also a source of information upon which differentiated instruction and feedback can be based. More on this topic in Chapters 5 and 12.

Becoming aware of how to personally master the content of learning is also closely related to assessment as learning, which is primarily designed to monitor progress through self-assessment, supporting learners to develop an awareness of their personal learning strategies and habits. It is associated with self-regulation, self-monitoring, metacognition, and feedback (Evans, 2013; Lysaght & O'Leary, 2013; Sadler, 2010). If learners cannot self-assess through assessment as learning, they cannot improve their learning to become expert learners. The relationship between expert learning and assessment is summarized in Figure 4.

Assessment for and assessment as learning are the principle mechanisms through which the supporting learning (Archer, 2017) purpose of assessment, described in Chapter 1, is fulfilled. Both mechanisms are covered in more detail in Chapter 5.

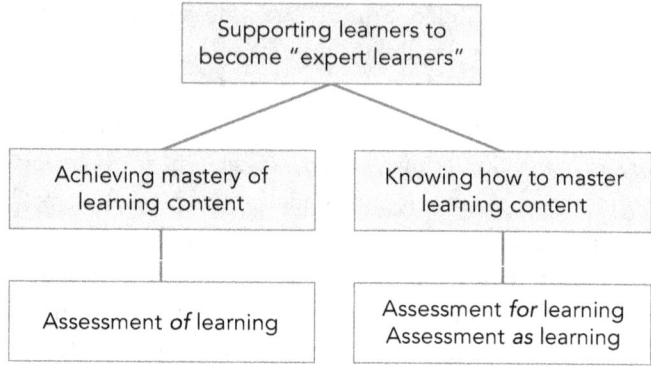

FIGURE 4: The relationship between expert learning and assessment

Due to their considerable variability, learners in higher education will differ in how they master the content of their learning, including how they demonstrate that they have mastered the content of their learning through assessment. Thus, we need to be flexible when it comes to the assessment process, as covered in Chapter 2.

Unfortunately, higher education has been almost entirely devoid of flexibility in terms of how learners achieve the goals of learning (through learning and teaching methods and resources) and demonstrate that achievement through assessment. Using assessments that erect barriers will seriously impede a learner's ability to demonstrate mastery over learning. As the quote (misattributed to Einstein) goes: "Everyone is a genius, but if you judge a fish by its ability to climb a tree, it will live its whole life believing that it is stupid."

In addition to its failure to embrace flexibility, another unfortunate characteristic of higher education has been its tendency to design barriers into the learning pathways learners navigate to achieve learning goals, including the assessments. These barriers are often inadvertent but in some circumstances are entirely intentional!

PAUSE AND THINK

- Do you currently use assessment for learning (formative assessment) strategies as part of your instructional experiences/teaching sessions? If not, can you find a way to include assessment for learning?

- Do you currently include opportunities for learners to self-assess and assess each other? How do your learners know what their learning strengths and areas for development are?

4

Assessment and the UDL Principles

Becoming an expert learner is related to three connected, interdependent neural networks in the brain known as the recognition, strategic, and affective networks (Rose & Meyer, 2002). These networks are represented by the UDL principles of representation, action and expression, and engagement, respectively, and learners are highly variable when it comes to them. When designing assessments, it is essential to consider how we can incorporate each UDL principle into the design.

Representation

The UDL framework recognizes that learners are variable in representation, or the "what" of learning, which relates to perceptions of language, symbols, and comprehension. Representation hugely influences the learning resources we create for our learners. For example, learners will differ in how they perceive and comprehend information related to learning. Some may cope well with text-based learning resources requiring them to read, whereas others may prefer using multimedia options such as a video or podcast.

Representation is sometimes described as providing "ways into content" (Hall et al., 2012). For a learner, an assessment—including the specific tasks, background information, instructions, and marking criteria—represents content they must learn. However, this assessment "content" has traditionally been presented in only one format: written text. Thus, if we want to embrace the representation principle in assessment design, we must provide multiple ways into the content of the assessment. For example, we could provide an assessment brief as a video or navigable web page.

Language is another critical issue when it comes to assessment. Frequently, assessment briefs contain lots of educational jargon. Teachers often assume that learners understand various assessment-related terms (such as brief, marking criteria, and rubric) when it's likely that some learners won't. Furthermore, we often assume that learners will understand the skills they'll be assessed on. For example, a learner may be asked to "critically evaluate," "differentiate," or "distinguish" as part of an essay, but they may not totally understand the meaning of such terms, especially in the context within which they must apply them. Therefore, we need to teach important terms; provide glossaries, language supports, and translation supports; and utilize images, videos, and other media to exemplify important assessment concepts. Assessment literacy isn't limited to knowing how to complete the assessment task.

When it comes to assessment, learners must make sense of the information presented to them and what they must do with it. This is why it is important that we supply and activate background knowledge. Maybe learners have been asked to "critically analyze" before on a different unit, so it's useful to remind them of that. We must show the big picture, demonstrating how what they've learned up to this point is relevant to the assessment, in a variety of ways and using a variety of tools, such as concept maps, visualizations, and graphic organizers.

Action and Expression

The UDL framework recognizes variability in action and expression, or the "how" of learning, relating to expression, communication, physical action, and executive function. The nature of action and expression means that it exerts an important influence on assessment, but the principle isn't simply about giving learners the choice between an essay or exam, for example. Sure, it is important for learners to have the option of demonstrating their learning in different formats, but it's not about offering 50 shades of written assessment.

Higher education has overwhelmingly relied on written demonstrations of learning (essay, exam, report, etc.) through the years, often failing to consider the relevance and authenticity of such methods. I inherited a teacher training course a few years ago in which the majority of assessments were essays. When does a teacher need to write an essay as part of their teaching practice? On one unit, an essay was replaced with a prerecorded screencast (or comparable alternative) created using the institutional lecture-capture software. It is mandatory to record lectures at my institution. Hence, the learners were getting important practice with the software as well as developing their ability to create asynchronous learning resources, which became essential during the COVID pandemic. The point is that the screencast not only was more occupationally relevant than the essay, but removed barriers for many of our largely international cohort who had demonstrated some challenges with writing fluently in English.

We must consider whether there are physical barriers in the assessment process. For example, will writing, typing, or speaking as part of an assessment be a barrier for any learner? In such scenarios, we should consider supportive technologies, such as providing the learner—who is better at orally articulating their ideas, as most of us tend to be—with speech-to-text software to help them more effectively plan an essay, for example. Supportive technologies aren't limited to learners with disabilities—everyone can benefit from them.

Can learners practice the skills required for successful assessment completion and develop fluency with them? For example, if the learners are to be assessed on their ability to "critically evaluate," can critical evaluation be practiced regularly as part of instruction? It's a real bugbear of mine how often learners are asked to demonstrate skills they haven't been given the opportunity to practice.

As the saying "you can't hit a target that you can't see" suggests, it's important to set goals as a means of planning intentioned actions. Learners should be supported in setting short-, medium-, and long-term assessment-related goals. Consider breaking down assessments into smaller parts or discrete tasks with goals set for completion, and providing learners with several strategies to complete their assessment so that they can choose the one that works best for them. There's not just one way to plan and write an essay, after all. Assessment literacy means supporting learners to develop their executive functioning skills too.

Engagement

The UDL framework recognizes variability in engagement, or the "why" of learning, which relates to learner interest, motivation, persistence, and self-regulation. There's nothing more demotivating than when learning lacks choice, ownership, relevance, and authenticity. Assessment tasks need to be meaningful, and we must make clear to learners why they are being assessed in a particular way, even in terms of how the assessment aligns to learning outcomes (more on those in Chapter 6). To that end, we can offer options for how an assessment will be completed. This might include the output, such as essay, poster, or presentation, as well as the content and the processes used to complete the assessment. As mentioned previously, a learner who finds word processing challenging could use speech-to-text software to plan and complete their essay instead, making the task more engaging for them. Or, for a presentation, we could give learners autonomy over the topic.

Learning is a journey and, like many journeys, it can be a long and arduous process at times. Long journeys can be made easier, however, if we set milestones. Reaching milestones provides us with essential feedback that we're on course to reach our destination, motivating us to persist. Learning is no different. Hence, it is important to give learners ongoing mastery-oriented feedback as "medals" (what they've done well and why) and "missions" (what they need to develop and how) as part of instruction and on formative and summative assessment, supporting their continued persistence with learning (Petty, 2014). *Agentic feedback*—feedback that promotes student agency by providing informative opportunities to revise understanding, as opposed to mere correction—may also be important in supporting learning (Griffiths et al., 2023) with potential motivational benefits.

Engagement has an emotional underpinning, and so emotion management through the development of self-regulation plays an important role in the assessment process. For example, it is important for learners to understand how they're feeling when assessment tasks are set. Motivated? Overwhelmed? Bored? We must intentionally support learners to recognize, manage, and use their emotions as they relate to assessment.

Supporting learners to recognize emotions could involve simply getting them to reflect on how they are feeling about an assessment. If those emotions are negative, you could ask learners to consider how they could manage those emotions, listing possible approaches as a means of broadening their toolkit of emotion management strategies. Finally, it can be useful to get learners to reflect on the optimal emotional state they require for assessment tasks. For example, if they need to read a lengthy book chapter in order to complete an assessment, what emotional state do they need to be in to read and absorb the information in the book successfully, and how can they induce that emotional state? Supporting learners to recognize, manage, and use their emotions—a topic we'll cover more in Chapter 7—raises their metacognitive awareness, supporting their ability to learn successfully.

PAUSE AND THINK

- How are you incorporating multiple means of representation into your assessments?

- How are you incorporating multiple means of action and expression into your assessments?

- How are you incorporating multiple means of engagement into your assessments?

5

Holistic Assessment Considerations

When contemplating a UDL assessment approach, it can be useful to think of assessment holistically by splitting assessment into three forms: assessment *of* learning, assessment *for* learning, and assessment *as* learning. When planning instruction, we should aim to develop assessment strategies that incorporate all three forms.

Assessment *of* Learning

Assessment *of* learning is summative assessment. As discussed in Chapter 3, summative assessment involves having a learner complete various performance tasks to assess the extent to which the learner understands the information, ideas, concepts, and skills that were taught during a unit of study and the extent to which they have achieved the learning goals for that unit. Summative assessments typically involve grading; are usually "high stakes" in that there are potential consequences for performing poorly, such as failing to achieve a passing or desired grade (Earl & Katz, 2006; Kibble, 2017); and are most closely associated with the certification, progress, and transfer purpose of assessment presented in Chapter 1. Stakeholders such as learners, parents, universities, teachers, and regulators may worry about the outcomes of summative assessment due to its "make or break" nature (Meyer et al., 2014). Some evidence suggests that the strong focus on summative assessment in educational settings has raised standards and achievement levels for learners (Phelps, 2005), while other research indicates that it causes teachers to "teach to the test," with the result that learners are engaging in less effective rote learning and failing to learn how to apply content in potentially meaningful ways (Supovitz, 2010).

As discussed in Chapter 4, assessments of learning should be designed with flexibility; variety; use of exemplars; marking descriptors; feed forward, the supply and activation of background knowledge and a clear brief; background information; and instructions (which may include language supports such as glossaries). Due to their high-stakes nature and centrality to learner motivation (Wormald et al., 2009), it is essential that they incorporate the UDL principles. They should also inform instructional design considerations. For example, since assessments of learning usually provide a measure of the extent to which learners have met the learning goals for a unit of study, it's critical that the goals created for individual instructional experiences directly align with the goals of the unit to which they belong (see Figure 5). Learners must be able to see how the learning they engage in during the instructional experience is directed toward and supports the completion of their assessments.

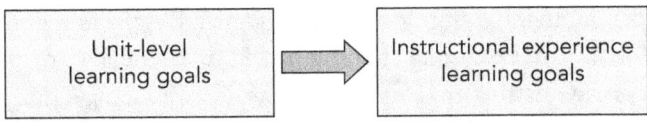

FIGURE 5: Alignment between learning goals of the unit of study and instructional experience

Furthermore, it is also critical that learners have the opportunity in class to demonstrate and practice the knowledge and skills that are being assessed. For a unit learning goal such as "By the conclusion of this unit, you will be able to distinguish between the learning theories of constructivism and behaviorism," for example, learners should be given the opportunity to practice—and receive feedback on—distinguishing between constructivism and behaviorism in class.

As critical as assessment of learning is in assessing the extent to which a learner understands the information, ideas, concepts, and skills taught during a unit of study, it can't be used to adapt or adjust instructional approaches for that unit because it generally occurs at the end of the unit, when instruction for the unit has finished (Connell, 2020). It is important to note that assessments from the UDL perspective are largely about assessing the effectiveness of the curriculum and instruction. Unfortunately, summative assessments are generally ineffective in this regard, focusing more on learner performance (Meyer et al., 2014).

Assessment *for* Learning

Assessment *for* learning is formative assessment. It supports teachers and learners in monitoring learning by gathering information on the progress learners are making. It can be highly intentioned and organized (e.g., assigning "work" that learners must complete periodically), or it can be unstructured and unplanned (e.g., noticing a puzzled look on a learner's face). In this respect, formative assessment exists along a continuum. At one end is *ad hoc* formative assessment, which is largely spontaneous, reactive, and intuitive, and at the other is *intentional* (by design) formative assessment, which is proactive and intentionally designed into the instructional experience (Connell, 2020). The point is that assessment for learning is a tool that uses information on learners to support instructional decision-making (Connell, 2020). The information derived from assessment for learning can provide learners with personalized direction about how they can achieve learning goals (Gardner, 2011), making this the most important type of assessment from a UDL perspective, and reflecting the UDL assessment principle that assessment is *ongoing and focused on learner progress* (Meyer et al., 2014).

A key function of assessment for learning is to provide ongoing feedback, helping learners identify strengths and areas for development to support them to accelerate their learning (Sadler, 1989). Feedback is usually qualitative in nature, incorporating agentic, dialogic, and feed-forward elements, as opposed to grades. Medals and missions (Petty, 2014), discussed in Chapter 4, are central feedback approaches with assessment for learning.

Formative assessments can be an effective way to prepare learners for summative assessments, since they provide an opportunity to practice, evaluate, and gain feedback on the knowledge and skills assessed as part of summative assessments. It is important that formative assessments are varied, include medals and missions in feedback, and give learners the opportunity to self-assess and peer-assess too. Many teachers feel unease at providing options and flexibility when it comes to assessments of learning. However, due to their relatively low-stakes nature, assessments for learning provide an ideal opportunity for options and flexibility, since their key purpose is to generate feedback.

> **PAUSE AND THINK**
>
> ☐ Do you currently use assessment for learning (formative assessment) strategies as part of your instructional experiences/ teaching sessions? If not, can you find a way to include it?

Information derived from assessments for learning can be used to provide differentiated instruction and feedback. For example, level of background knowledge of a topic is an important source of variability among learners, but many teachers are unaware of their learners' background knowledge because they don't assess it. A formative diagnostic assessment of background knowledge can help them work out which learners require additional scaffolds and supports, and which require additional stretch and challenge (more on the diagnostic use of assessment for learning in Chapter 11). As Michael Connell states in his great book *Using Formative Assessment to Improve Student Outcomes in Classrooms*, unlike summative assessment, which looks backward to take a snapshot of capability in a given domain, formative assessment is forward-looking and used intentionally to adapt instruction and better support learning toward a specific end goal (Connell, 2020).

Assessment for learning should be an inherent part of instruction. It is critical that learners understand their progress, their strengths, and the skills they need to develop. Similarly, teachers require information to modify their teaching approaches as well as to provide differentiated instruction and feedback. Assessment for learning aids each of these processes. As noted in Chapter 3, it supports learners to become expert learners, particularly the aspect of expert learning that involves learners knowing how to personally master learning content.

Assessment *as* Learning

Assessment as learning is a variation of formative assessment that essentially consists of self-assessment and reflection. Its primary purpose is to support learners to monitor their progress and develop an awareness of their personal learning habits and strategies. Assessment as learning supports metacognitive development; it is associated with self-regulation, self-monitoring, metacognition, and feedback (Evans, 2013; Lysaght & O'Leary, 2013; Sadler, 2010). It enables learners to become proactive and skilled in monitoring their own learning and to develop greater understanding of the methods and materials that support their learning (Meyer et al., 2014). Assessment as learning reflects a key UDL assessment principle in that it *involves and informs learners* (Meyer et al., 2014).

Learners should be encouraged to develop their capability to self-assess, as a means of becoming aware of the strategies and approaches that help them to study and learn most effectively. An important part of understanding how to study and learn effectively involves supporting learners to understand their personal motivations for study and learning. For example, recognition of such issues can support learners to develop confidence, take risks, stretch, grow, and develop the self-regulation and independence required for higher education study.

A critical capability in higher education is the ability to self-direct learning and study independently. Assessment as learning serves the important function of assisting learners in establishing a stronger understanding of their progress and of how well they are getting on as independent learners. When learners clearly understand the knowledge, skills, and abilities they must develop, they also become more aware of the support and development they require and better equipped to pursue whatever tools and supports they need to optimize their learning and subsequent achievement. Typical assessment as learning tasks include learners engaging in self and peer review (Sadler, 2009) or using exemplars to assess theirs and others' work (Carless et al., 2011).

Like assessment for learning, assessment as learning plays a pivotal role in developing the aspects of expert learning, especially those that focus on learners being able to personally master learning content through the development of metacognitive skills. It is difficult for learners to improve their level of learning if they cannot self-assess; hence, assessment as learning is a critical ingredient in the design of instructional experiences.

PAUSE AND THINK

- Do you currently include opportunities for learners to self-assess and assess each other?

- How do your learners know what their learning strengths and areas for development are?

Part II

Assessment Design

6

Learning Outcomes and Assessment

So what exactly are learning outcomes? Quite simply, a learning outcome provides learners with information about what they must know or be able to do as a result of their learning, whether in the context of an entire program, a unit of study, or a single instructional experience. Outcomes provide the goals upon which learners can focus strategic actions.

It can be useful to think of learning outcomes as the destination point for a journey. If we're in the car traveling but don't have a clear destination, we're just driving around aimlessly, not knowing where we're going, how to get there, or how long it'll take. Likewise, if there is nothing to direct learning toward, then it is effectively aimless and unfocused. Because they provide strategic direction for learning, learning outcomes are a critical aspect of backward design (Wiggins & McTighe, 2005). Once we know where we want to go, we can work backward to create a pathway to get there.

Measuring Learning Outcomes

Whatever it is that learners are expected to know or be able to do as a result of their learning, there should always be a mechanism for measuring the extent to which they know or can do it. In this respect, a critical feature of learning outcomes from an assessment perspective is that they are measurable. For this reason, we must be careful when creating learning outcomes. It's unhelpful to create a learning outcome related to what a learner will *understand* by the conclusion of a unit of learning, for example, because understanding a concept can be defined in a variety of ways—from simply describing it to the more complex cognitive process of critically analyzing it—and is thus difficult to measure. Therefore, it is essential that the outcome clearly frames how learners can demonstrate their understanding so that measurement can happen more effectively.

Let's take this example: "This unit will help you to understand the anatomy of the heart." This is not a very good learning outcome because understand is vague and we don't know what it means in this context. It's impossible to actually measure whether learners have achieved the required level of understanding, because we're not clear on what the required level of understanding is.

Now consider this example: "By the end of this unit, you will be able to label the major anatomic structures found in the human heart."

This is better, because the way learners demonstrate their understanding—by labeling the human heart's major anatomical structures—is clear. This learning outcome is straightforward to measure: we simply set a task to have learners label a diagram of the heart.

This measurable aspect to a learning outcome is known as the *assessment construct*—what specifically an assessment intends to measure (see Figure 6). If we say an assessment has construct relevance, we're saying that the assessment is a genuine measure of what it intends to measure, like the heart labeling task. Indeed, a key UDL assessment principle is that assessments are construct relevant (Meyer et al., 2014).

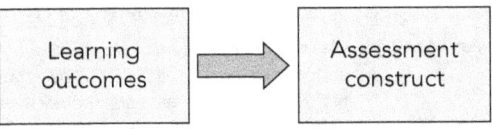

FIGURE 6: Learning outcomes give rise to the assessment construct.

However, assessments sometimes include *irrelevant constructs*—aspects of the assessment that are unintentionally measured. For example, when a learner takes an exam, their knowledge of the exam subject is being measured, but so is their handwriting if the exam is handwritten (as many still are). Irrelevant constructs are discussed in more detail in Chapter 7.

Table 1 offers some tips for creating effective learning outcomes.

 PAUSE AND THINK

- How well written are your learning outcomes? Do they have a clear assessment construct?

Table 1: Top Tips for Creating Effective Learning Outcomes

Use future tense.	Always use the future tense—for example, "By the end of this session/block of learning, you will be able to _____."
Reflect the most important information/content.	It is tempting to base your teaching purely on content. However, the key question to ask yourself is: *What do I want the learners to learn or be able to do by the end of the program/module/session/unit of learning?* Asking this question will help you identify the most important information that the learners must learn and then base the learning outcomes on that content.
Make goals SMART.	Make sure the outcomes are clear, with no ambiguity. Can they realistically be achieved in the given timeframe, and are they measurable as part of a knowledge check or check for understanding? Keep your learners in mind when you write learning outcomes. When writing learning outcomes, use the acronym SMART: Specific, Measurable, Achievable, Realistic, and Timely.
Use straightforward language.	Use straightforward language and avoid jargon. A learner will have a much higher likelihood of achieving a learning outcome if they understand what it means and what is being asked of them.
Include process outcomes as well as product outcomes.	A common pitfall when writing learning outcomes is to reflect only the tangible aspects of learning, such as the end product of the assessment process. For example, instead of having an outcome that states "By the end of the module, you will be able to write a laboratory report," it would be better to state "By the end of the module, you will be able to devise, write, and implement a laboratory report." The second outcome is more useful because it provides clear information on the process the learners must follow to complete the assessment, not just the end product of the assessment.
Pitch at the appropriate level.	Make sure outcomes are pitched at the appropriate academic level.

Table 1: Top Tips for Creating Effective Learning Outcomes *(continued)*

Include multiple outcome types.	When writing learning outcomes, include a balance of different outcome types, including knowledge-, application-, and skills-based outcomes.
Separate learning outcomes from the means of achieving them.	Learning outcomes in higher education are often fixed and non-negotiable. However, the means of achieving them can be entirely flexible. For example, an outcome might be: "Discuss the pros and cons of the UK leaving the European Union." Achieving this outcome could take many forms, such as an essay, conversation, presentation, debate, or poster. There is rarely only one way to achieve an outcome.

Dissecting Learning Outcomes

When supporting learners to demonstrate their capability to know or do whatever is stipulated in learning outcomes, it can be useful to dissect the learning outcomes into their constituent parts. Generally, learning outcomes will consist of two key aspects: a skill (can be practical or cognitive) and some content to which the skill is applied.

Let's use this example: "By the conclusion of this unit, you will be able to **critically evaluate** the impact of **Brexit** on the **UK economy**." I've highlighted the cognitive skills and content in bold. In this scenario, learners must apply the cognitive skill (critical evaluation) to the content (the impact of Brexit on the UK economy). Before they can critically evaluate the impact of Brexit on the UK economy, they first must know something about Brexit and its impact on the UK economy.

Thus, our first step as teachers is to think about how we could supply the content knowledge that learners must know in order to apply the cognitive skill and achieve the outcome. Although this may sound obvious, I've seen plenty of instances where teachers teach topics that they enjoy, are comfortable with, or have researched but that are only partially relevant to the content requirements of the outcome. Remember, the starting point for design is always the outcome, never the content. First, we articulate what the learners are required to know or do, and this drives the content. We shouldn't be arbitrarily selecting topics to teach from our favorite textbook!

The next step is to think about how learners could develop the skill of critical evaluation. You should make every effort to explicitly teach that skill, providing learners with opportunities to practice it in class and to receive feedback on their application of it. It could also be advantageous to formatively assess their capability to apply the skill. In my previous book, *Delivering Inclusive and Impactful Instruction* (2023), I drew on Geoff Petty's EDUCARE? mnemonic (Petty, 2014) as a means of teaching complex cognitive skills like critical evaluation. Table 2 summarizes that approach.

PAUSE AND THINK

- Do you intentionally and explicitly teach complex skills, particularly cognitive ones, to your learners?

- Do your learners get the opportunity to practice their application of complex cognitive skills before they are assessed on them?

Table 2: The EDUCARE? Approach to Mastering Skills (Adapted From Petty, 2014)

E	Explain	Explain to the learners the skill being taught. What does it mean? Why is it important? Why do they need to learn it?
D	Demonstrate	Demonstrate the skill for learners. It is important that they see how to do the skill before they attempt it themselves.
U	Use	Give learners the opportunity to use or practice the skill through learning activities of their choice.
C	Check and correct	Check and correct learners' practice of the skill and provide feedback with medals (what they did well and why) and missions (what they can improve and how).
A	Aide memoir	Provide learners with a reminder or summary of the key points relating to the skill and its application.
R	Review	Give learners consistent opportunities to review and reuse the skills they've learned to ensure continued proficiency in their application of those skills.
E	Evaluate	Give learners the opportunity to demonstrate their learning to ensure that they have learned the skill correctly.
?	Questions	Provide multiple opportunities for learners to ask questions during their learning of the skill.

7

Assessment Barriers

UDL is essentially about removing or reducing environmental barriers to learning, including the demonstration of learning through assessment. Unfortunately, the construction of many assessments occurs in such a way that barriers are frequently designed into them, including the processes for completing them. Sometimes barriers are so prevalent in assessment that the process becomes less about legitimately and authentically demonstrating learning, and more about navigating the various barriers.

When considering assessment barriers, it is useful to think about the UDL principles. For example, barriers may be due to the lack of multiple means of engagement, representation, and action and expression in the assessment process. It may be helpful to review Chapter 4 to examine how the UDL principles remove barriers. For the remainder of this chapter, we'll explore in further detail some of the most common assessment barriers, although keep in mind it is not an exhaustive list.

Irrelevant Constructs

Irrelevant constructs are perhaps the most common barriers to effective assessment. They're literally everywhere and frequently teachers simply aren't aware of them. Let's return to the exam example from Chapter 6, which described how, whenever a learner takes a handwritten exam, not only is their knowledge of the exam subject being measured, but so is their handwriting. In addition, if the exam were unseen (learners don't know the questions in advance), closed book (learners are not permitted to use resources such as notes or textbooks), and timed, then it would also be measuring time management, working memory, and organizational skill. Each of these irrelevant constructs could represent barriers for some learners. As a result, the skill learned in successfully completing the assessment isn't in the demonstration of learning by answering the exam questions correctly but in successfully navigating all the barriers!

Time is a frequent assessment barrier, particularly when it comes to exams or tests. Sometimes it's necessary for learners to demonstrate their learning under time-sensitive conditions. For example, a nurse being assessed on their ability to administer CPR may be assessed under time-constrained conditions, since in a real setting, failing to administer CPR in a timely manner might mean someone dies. In this scenario, the time-constrained assessment is occupationally relevant. However, for an exam question like "Discuss the social and political impact of the American Civil War," imposing a time constraint would not be relevant to the assessment. A learner could—and should be allowed to—take all the time they need to plan and compose an answer to this prompt that clearly demonstrates their learning.

Requiring learners to manage their time is frequently an irrelevant construct. If a learner requests extra time to complete an assessment (as is frequently the case for learners taking exams and tests), then it's safe to say that time is a barrier. In this instance, giving a learner extra time is akin to giving them a ladder to climb a wall—but what we should be doing is thinking of ways to break down the wall altogether. As mentioned in Chapter 2, some learners are disadvantaged by time constraints but aren't permitted extra time. This is all the more reason to rethink the assessment process altogether.

Sometimes the assessment method itself can represent an irrelevant construct. For example, let's say learners have been given a live presentation task to assess their capability to achieve this learning outcome from the previous chapter: "By the conclusion of this unit, you will be able to critically evaluate the impact of Brexit on the UK economy." First, is a live presentation task the only way learners can demonstrate their ability to critically evaluate the impact of Brexit on the UK economy? No—there are literally dozens of other ways for them to do so. Giving them options for how they can demonstrate this capability will support engagement and remove barriers. For example, some learners might find live presentations difficult because they are non-native English speakers, have an anxiety disorder, or live far from campus, making it difficult for them to attend on the day of presentation. Allowing them to choose how to demonstrate their new skill in the way they're most comfortable with will support their interest, motivation, and perseverance with the assessment task.

Second, if the learners are assessed on their presentation skills or the attractiveness of their presentation materials (as frequently occurs in such scenarios), then irrelevant constructs are being assessed; nowhere in the learning outcome does it state that they will demonstrate the capability to present well or produce attractive presentation resources. The learners must demonstrate only their capability to critically evaluate how Brexit has impacted the UK economy. They could give a poor presentation, with no resources, and still demonstrate this capability effectively. Similar issues frequently arise in written assessments where learners are penalized for writing style, spelling, referencing, and the like, when none of the aforementioned constructs is relevant to the outcome or capability they must demonstrate.

PAUSE AND THINK

- Take a look at your assessments. Are there any irrelevant constructs?

Information and Instructions

Information relating to assessments, including background, context, a statement of the task, and practical instructions for completion (such as word count, format, and marking criteria) are frequently presented to learners in some sort of assessment brief. Assessment briefs were introduced in Chapter 4, which discussed the role they play in developing learner assessment literacy.

Assessment briefs can present several representation barriers because they are often provided in a limited (written) format, with few alternative options. Furthermore, they frequently contain language likely to be unfamiliar to learners, such as terms concerning the skills or abilities learners must demonstrate as part of the assessment (e.g., "critically analyze," "differentiate," or "appraise") or "teacher language" (e.g., "marking criteria" or "rubric"). Too many assessment briefs are created with the assumption that learners will understand these terms—and with few if any supports, such as glossaries, provided to help them. As a result, navigating the assessment brief can be challenging simply due to the language it uses. Perhaps Derek Rowntree (2015) put it best when he stated that assessment is characterized by "conceptual quagmires and terminological traps."

Another potential barrier within the assessment brief is the assessment instructions—what the learners are actually required to do. This involves the presentation of the assessment construct and the expected means by which learners will respond. For example, they may be given an essay to write in response to a question, but do they need to provide an introduction, review of literature, conclusion, or something else? How many words does each section need to be, and how is it weighted in terms of the marking criteria? There's nothing more frustrating than turning in a brilliant introduction that took ages to write, only to find it's worth just 10% of the overall grade for the essay! How much easier would it be to create a strategy for completing the essay if it were clear that the majority of the marks were for the main body? Also, what referencing system is being used, when is the work due, and where and how should it be submitted? These may seem like obvious questions, but believe me, they're not always answered clearly for learners. Just because you understand the brief doesn't mean your learners will. For these reasons, it can be useful to get review and feedback on your assessment briefs before you use them with learners.

Irrespective of how well constructed a brief is, it should be used in class as an instructional tool, part of a shared dialogue with learners in which agentic exploration can take place. Remember that assessment is perhaps the most anxiety-inducing aspect of learning, so learners must have opportunities to "unpack" and make sense of the brief in class. Assessment briefs are elements of the assessment process that must be learnable to learners—that learners must make sense of and respond to—so it's critical we support them to do so.

Perhaps one of the most dangerous assumptions we make when it comes to assessment is that learners possess the know-how or tacit knowledge required to complete assessments effectively. Tacit knowledge is largely gained through personal experience and context. However, learners from international settings—with experience of different educational systems, for example—may not possess this know-how.

If the task of an assessment is understanding what the task actually is because the information and instructions are so poor, this is a large barrier. Such issues are perhaps best explained by *cognitive load theory (CLT)*, which posits that learners' information processing and knowledge construction capabilities can be impeded by the cognitive load of other learning tasks (Sweller et al., 2019). For example, unnecessary tasks and distractions can increase cognitive load to the point that learning and transfer are diminished (Sweller et al., 2019). In the assessment context, this means that if we create poor assessment instructions that learners must "decipher," we're ramping up the cognitive load and compromising their ability to focus on the task itself.

Furthermore, instructors should aim to promote germane cognitive load that supports the construction of schemas (Sweller et al., 1998). Schemas form from materials learned through instruction and reflect how learners organize, structure, and store information for learning (Morales-Martinez et al., 2021), including that for assessment. Hence, with well-constructed and consistent assessment information and instructions, extraneous cognitive load is prevented and germane load is promoted through schema development.

Social and Emotional Barriers

Many assessments erect emotional barriers—for example, most of us feel anxious when taking exams, giving presentations, or being "interrogated" during an oral exam. Thus, it might be necessary to offer a range of assessment methods for learners who may experience debilitating negative emotions. Remember, if learners are being asked to give a presentation and the presentation skills themselves aren't part of the assessment construct, then the presentation element is an irrelevant construct and possible barrier.

Sometimes it's not possible to use an alternative assessment method, however, as is frequently the case for skills- or competency-based assessments (discussed in Chapter 8). Thus, in addition to removing irrelevant constructs from assessments, it is important to encourage learners to develop coping skills and strategies that help them self-regulate their emotions during an anxiety-inducing assessment.

Developing coping strategies and self-regulation skills could involve some simple exercises rooted in emotional intelligence (EI) skills training (Brackett & Katulak, 2007) that get learners to recognize how they're feeling—and the intensity of that feeling—in relation to assessment. Learners could then be encouraged to write down how they currently manage their negative emotions about assessment, how successful that strategy is, and what else they could do to manage their negative emotions. They could also be encouraged to identify the optimal emotional state they would need to be in to do well in the assessment, and to think of strategies to help them elicit that state (Brackett & Katulak, 2007). Tables 3 through 5 show some templates to help learners self-regulate their emotions about assessment.

Emotional Skills Training Templates

Table 3: Recognizing Emotion Activity Template

RECOGNIZING EMOTION	
Learning event, situation, or activity?	**How were you feeling? How strong were those feelings on a scale of 1-10?**
My teacher provided us with our assessment task for this unit, due in three weeks' time.	I was feeling anxious because I am required to give a presentation as part of the assessment. I would say the intensity of the feeling is about 8.

Table 4: Managing Emotion Activity Template

MANAGING EMOTION
What is the emotion?
Anxiety and a little bit of fear.
What triggers the emotion?
Whenever I get asked to give a presentation, it makes me anxious and a bit scared because I've never been very good at presentations and usually do badly.
How do you currently manage/deal with the emotion?
I just force myself into giving the presentation despite feeling anxious.
How effective is your current strategy for managing the emotion?
Not very effective. I've never got a grade above 50% for a presentation.
What else could you do to manage the emotion?
I could practice in front of friends, and maybe break the task down into smaller chunks, so just present the introduction and then on a different day present the main body, etc.

Table 5: Using Emotion Activity Template

USING EMOTION		
The learning environment and its effect on me		
I don't like being asked to read silently in class. I feel under pressure to read as quickly as everyone else and it makes me conscious that I'm a slow reader. It also distracts me and so I can't extract what I need from the reading.		
How can I generate the right mood for study?		
I want to be in the right emotional state to read important passages of text and absorb the key information, as I need the information for my assessments.		
Activity	**Desired state**	**How to generate**
Reading	Relaxed and focused	Find a quiet space to read with no distractions and comfortable furniture. Make sure I have food and water so that I don't get hungry or thirsty during my reading. Make sure I have lots of time in case I have to reread certain passages or need time to make sense of them. I don't want to be rushed. Allow myself time to take a break if I start to flag. Give myself the reward of a milkshake afterward for finishing the task.

8

Assessing Knowledge and Skills

Generally speaking, a UDL approach to assessment encourages options and choices when it comes to the ways in which learners demonstrate their learning. Sometimes teachers may offer an alternative assessment option (e.g., essay or presentation) or even several possible assessment options (e.g., essay, presentation, or oral exam), but many feel uneasy and perhaps a little daunted by offering options and choices when it comes to assessment due to concerns about equivalence, rigor, fairness, and accuracy.

An exasperated teacher once said to me in a workshop, "Surely a piece of interpretive dance can't be offered as an alternative to an essay?!" This example highlights a common misconception many teachers hold when it comes to offering assessment options with UDL—that we simply allow learners to be assessed however they want. This of course isn't true. Any options offered to learners will be based on what is being assessed, which in turn will naturally influence how it is assessed. For example, interpretive dance would not really work as an alternative to an essay if history knowledge were being assessed; although no doubt entertaining, the piece of dance would not permit a learner to demonstrate their achievement of the learning outcomes. Thinking about what is being assessed brings us back to the assessment construct, which stems directly from the learning outcomes. Any options and choices must provide a genuine measure of the assessment construct.

Sometimes, despite being able to clearly locate the assessment construct, you might encounter instances where providing assessment options is both challenging and not necessarily appropriate. A useful way to approach this situation is to first determine whether the assessment is predominantly assessing skills and competencies or knowledge.

Assessing Skills and Competencies

In some circumstances, learners will be assessed on their ability to demonstrate various skills and competencies. Often, these are applied or practical skills that are highly relevant to a particular vocation or job role. Skill- and competency-based assessments enable learners to demonstrate that they can perform the skills or competencies at some required or threshold level that qualifies them to perform those skills in a real-world context. For example, the practical element of a driving test works this way. Once a learner driver has met the threshold for a passing score on their test, they may legally drive a car.

Due to the nature of skills and competencies, there tends to be little flexibility in terms of assessment method, making it difficult to provide options. For example, imagine you are enrolled in a public speaking course. The only real, valid, and relevant assessment for such a course would be some sort of public speaking task, because public speaking is the skill being assessed. Writing an essay on public speaking or creating a poster wouldn't enable you to demonstrate that you can perform the skill of public speaking. Similarly, a driving test could not consist solely of the theory test that learner drivers must take, since, in isolation, it does not assess how competently learners can drive a car.

Skills- and competency-based assessments tend to have high construct relevance as well as a high level of authenticity and occupational relevance built in. Although there is less opportunity to provide assessment options when assessing skills and competencies, there are still numerous ways in which you can make them more accessible and inclusive. Continuing with the public speaking course example, although there's little leeway in the nature of the task itself, the topic of your speech can be entirely flexible; that is, you should be able to select the topic, since this personalizes the assessment and thus makes it more engaging.

You should also have different options around how to approach the public speaking task. For example, there isn't just one way to plan, design, and deliver a public speaking engagement; there are many possibilities, such as a narrative storytelling approach, a visual or freeform approach, or even a PechaKucha-style (a presentation comprising 20 slides that are each displayed for only 20 seconds) approach. Learners should be given a range of approaches and select which works best for them.

Assessing Knowledge

Learners are frequently asked to demonstrate their knowledge of various topics and concepts through assessment. Sometimes they may be required to provide different types of knowledge (factual, conceptual, procedural, metacognitive) as well as to apply different types of thinking skills to those types of knowledge (classification, analysis, evaluation, etc.). For example, an assessment task might ask learners to "differentiate (analysis) between the learning theories of constructivism and behaviorism (conceptual knowledge)." Traditionally in higher education, learners are asked to demonstrate their learning in a scenario like this as some form of written communication, such as an essay or exam. However, it's clear that the ability to differentiate between the two theories is not limited to writing about them. Learners could give a presentation, create a poster, record a video, record a podcast, or even participate in an oral exam and still demonstrate their learning appropriately. The assessment construct is broad enough to enable multiple means of assessment. Based on the construct, the same marking criteria could even be used across different assessment types.

Unlike assessing skills, which tends to be highly construct relevant, assessing knowledge often comes with the potential for irrelevant constructs. For example, if learners were required to differentiate between constructivism and behaviorism by writing an essay, then they'd also be being assessed on irrelevant factors such as their ability to communicate in writing, structure an essay, and spell and reference correctly as well as several other constructs. When assessing knowledge, it's critical to look out for irrelevant constructs and try to remove or reduce them.

A final important consideration when deciding on options for assessing knowledge is authenticity. Whatever method or methods you choose, it is important that they represent an authentic measure of the assessment construct as well as occupational authenticity. For example, it makes more sense for health care professionals to demonstrate their biology knowledge in consultation with a patient as opposed to in an exam. Occupational authenticity provides a realistic preview of the types of knowledge demonstration that learners may engage with in their careers.

PAUSE AND THINK

- Are your assessments primarily assessing various forms of knowledge or skills and competencies?

9

Evaluating Your Assessments

As with all aspects of learning and teaching practice, creating accessible, inclusive, and equitable assessments that provide a clear, occupationally relevant measure of intended learning goals is a learnable skill. Thus, you can improve your assessments by intentionally trying to make them better, and this is where assessment evaluation comes in. Teachers should make an effort to evaluate the assessments they use, whether those are assessments they've used for a number of years or brand-new ones they're planning to use in the future. The purpose of evaluating an assessment is essentially to "unpick" your assessment design to help you better understand how well the assessment measures intended learning goals and whether that measurement is impeded by any environmental barriers.

When evaluating your assessments, it can be useful to start with the following three questions, which I have adapted from the work of Posey and Bastoni (2021):

How do I make sure my assessments are linked to the intended learning goals?

In Chapter 6, we explored the measurable aspect of learning goals or outcomes, known as the assessment construct—that which an assessment intends to measure. This is exactly what we're talking about when we talk about our assessments being linked to the intended learning goals. Does your assessment possess construct relevance—in other words, is it a genuine measure of what it intends to measure?

How do my assessments get learners interested?

Chapter 4 explored the place of the UDL principles in assessment design. The engagement principle in particular is about interest, motivation, persistence, and self-regulation, so we're thinking primarily about engaging learners through assessment at this point. It is important to reflect on whether your assessments allow choice, ownership, relevance, and authenticity, as well as whether they represent interesting and meaningful tasks for learners, with a clear rationale. Sometimes you can stimulate interest by offering options for assessment "output"; for example, some learners may much prefer recording a video over writing an essay. For some learners, interest may develop iteratively as the process of putting their assessment together unfolds. For example, interim formative feedback that lets a learner know where they are relative to an upcoming summative assessment can be a powerful motivating force. Supporting learners to regulate their emotions around assessment, especially if the process becomes challenging or anxiety inducing, can support motivation, effort, and persistence. In addition to the assessment method itself, will the *process* learners go through to complete an assessment generate and maintain interest, motivation, and persistence?

What barriers might learners experience when completing my assessments?

Chapter 7 explored assessment barriers, focusing on irrelevant constructs, information and instruction barriers, and social and emotional barriers. Remember from that discussion that you must scan your assessments for potential barriers, which are most often due to irrelevant constructs (unintended measures). Is your assessment measuring anything that could impede successful demonstration of the learning goals? For example, if the goal of the assessment is to demonstrate biology knowledge, does sitting down in an exam hall and having to handwrite answers to unseen questions, with no supporting resources, for four hours, potentially impede learner demonstration of the learning goals? (I'll let you answer that one for yourself!)

One possible way to address potential barriers in your assessments is to take the following steps (also adapted from the work of Posey and Bastoni, 2021), which essentially break down how learners are presented with, interact with, and respond to the assessment construct:

1. Examine your construct presentation.

Take a look at your assessment brief, background information, and/or instructions. Is the assessment clearly linked to the learning goal(s)? Is the assessment construct clear to the learner? Do they know clearly which knowledge skills and/or abilities are being assessed? Are there any barriers? For example, have you asked them to demonstrate a particular skill, such as a cognitive one like critical analysis? Are you sure that the learners understand what "critical analysis" means?

2. Consider your construct interaction.

How are the learners required to interact with the construct? How is the construct being presented to them? Do they have to answer a question? Do they have to read? Do they have to look at an image? Do they have to watch a video? What is the stimulus that they must comprehend and act upon? Are there any barriers? For example, are you asking a learner with dyslexia or non-native English speaker to read lengthy quantities of text with no alternative options?

3. Evaluate the learner response.

How do learners interact with the construct? What is it they are required to do to demonstrate the knowledge or skills and abilities being assessed? Are they writing, speaking, presenting, or demonstrating? Are they required to engage with irrelevant constructs that could be barriers? Are they being assessed on anything that is not part of the assessment construct? Are there any barriers? For example, is a learner who handwrites slowly and spells poorly being asked to handwrite with accuracy for several hours? Is there a possible alternative?

PAUSE AND THINK

- Grab one of your summative assessments. Use the information and guidance provided in this chapter to evaluate it. Do you need to make changes?

Part III

Putting It All Together

10

Bringing Assessment Into the Classroom

There are often two parallel worlds in higher education: the world of instruction, which takes place in class and where teachers (usually) broadcast content for learners to absorb and hopefully make sense of, and the world of assessment, which takes place outside of the classroom during self-directed study time and is usually solely the learner's responsibility. You probably realize by now that I don't think this is a great model. Sure, teachers may spend a session or so explaining the assessment to their learners, but this "explaining" often repeats what learners could find out for themselves on a well-constructed assessment brief. Indeed, the fact that teachers need to explain the task at all perhaps hints at some flaws in the assessment design process.

While I am not totally against teachers providing further explanation of assessment tasks to learners (it is "multiple means," after all), I am a firm believer that assessment must be a much more prominent part of instruction. The high-stakes nature of assessment, with its potential consequences for poor performance (Earl & Katz, 2006; Kibble, 2017), means it is often central to learner motivation (Wormald et al., 2009) and perhaps one of the most anxiety-inducing elements of the learning experience. Thus, it makes sense to make assessment a central part of instruction, and this chapter will provide some practical ideas for how you can do so.

Evaluate Instructional Goals

As Chapters 2 and 5 explained, individual instructional experiences or teaching sessions should have clear learning goals or outcomes—what learners should know or be able to do as a result of their participation in that learning experience. Those instructional goals provide strategic direction for learning, are a critical aspect of backward design (Wiggins & McTighe, 2005), and should align with the overall goals for the unit or module (refer back to Figure 5 in Chapter 5). Since summative assessment usually takes place at the unit or module level, when instructional goals are aligned to unit/module goals, it's much clearer to learners how instruction supports assessment. Furthermore, those instructional goals should themselves be assessed, since it is critical to know whether your learners know what they need to know or can do what they need to be able to do following an instructional experience. Otherwise, how will you know if your teaching has been effective? It is also critical for learners, because when instructional goals match unit/module goals and are assessed, learners get a barometer of their progress toward those unit/module goals on which they will be summatively assessed.

Approach Assessment Holistically

As discussed in Chapter 5, it is important to approach assessment holistically, incorporating assessment *of*, *for*, and *as* learning approaches into your practice. As well as aligning instructional goals to unit/module goals to support assessment *of* learning (summative assessment) as previously detailed, it is useful to provide time in class for learners to work on assessment of learning tasks. Assessment *for* learning (formative assessment) can be used to differentiate instruction and feedback, modify teaching approaches, and provide learners with critical feedback on how they're progressing toward learning goals. Finally, assessment *as* learning (self-assessment and reflection) can help learners monitor their progress and develop awareness of their personal learning habits and strategies, and it also supports metacognitive development since it relates to self-regulation, self-monitoring, metacognition, and feedback (Evans, 2013; Lysaght & O'Leary, 2013; Sadler, 2010). Typical assessment as learning tasks might include learners engaging in self- and peer review of class work (Sadler, 2009) or using exemplars to assess their own and others' work (Carless et al., 2011).

Use Diagnostic Assessment

Diagnostic assessment will be covered in the next chapter, but I'll touch on it briefly here. One important source of learner variability is their prior knowledge and understanding of the topic you're about to teach them. Some may have well-developed knowledge, understanding, and experience of the topic, whereas others may have none.

Thus, performing an early diagnostic assessment of prior learning can be an effective way to provide more personalized instruction, differentiate instruction and feedback, and raise learners' awareness of their strengths and gaps, helping you meet learners where they are, not where you hoped they'd be.

Have Learners Assess and Give Feedback to Each Other

It is often said that the best way to learn anything is to teach it to someone else; indeed, there are significant potential benefits in learners assessing and giving feedback to each other. Assessment and feedback are essential elements of teaching and two critical elements of Phil Race's (2019) "ripples on a pond" model of how learners really learn. Learners should be given opportunities to assess their own and their peers' learning through self-assessment tasks, peer-supported study, and various evaluation activities and feedback. Being able to assess one's own and others' learning and to apply criteria to evidence learning supports critical judgment making, in turn supporting deep learning (Race, 2019).

In my book *Delivering Inclusive and Impactful Instruction* (2023), I introduced the Roadmap for Teaching, shown in Figure 7, as a way to incorporate opportunities for assessment (evaluation) and feedback into your instruction.

The roadmap contains four critical elements: learning outcomes or goals, learning activities, evaluation activities, and opportunities for feedback. Feedback can be applied formatively at two critical points: when the learners are engaging in learning activities, and upon completion of evaluation activities.

Learning Outcomes	Learning Activities	Evaluation Activities
Outline what the learner will be able to do by the end of the teaching session, reflecting skills in Bloom's taxonomy.	These should directly reflect the learning outcomes and provide an opportunity to practice Bloom's skills.	These should also directly reflect the learning outcomes and provide an opportunity to evaluate whether learners have achieved the learning outcomes.

Feedback Opportunity 1	Feedback Opportunity 2
Supports learners to interpret and use skills correctly, providing critical information on correct practice, errors, and omissions.	Supports learners to interpret and use skills, correctly providing critical information on correct practice, errors, and omissions.

FIGURE 7: The Roadmap for Teaching

Familiarize Learners With Assessment

It is important to intentionally acquaint learners with their summative assessments instead of relying on them to do so themselves. Consider presenting the assessment brief, background instructions, and marking criteria in the classroom at each session and using them as a point of reference when covering key learning points. The brief background instructions and marking criteria could potentially be used as instructional tools. The brief and other elements will usually be placed somewhere on a learning management system (LMS); however, some learners may prefer to have a physical handout of these materials—and this of course supports multiple means. One teacher I know created posters of his summative assessment brief and posted them on the classroom walls to use as a teaching tool and an important reminder to learners.

I've already mentioned the need to create very clear assessment briefs, background instructions, and marking criteria. Remember, the assessment task should never be to work out what the task is! When learners have to "decode" their assessment tasks, it places an extraneous cognitive load on them— cognitive effort that could and should be spent learning content and developing important skills. To prevent extraneous cognitive load, consider whether your assessment asks learners to do something they may be unfamiliar with (e.g., "critically analyze," "distinguish," "differentiate," "appraise," "hypothesize") and clarify important assessment-related words, phrases, and expectations. Don't assume that all learners understand these terms or that they can all perform such skills. Support learners to develop their capabilities with these skills.

You can also ask your learners to "flip the feedback": Provide them with an example of a completed summative assessment they will undertake later in their unit or module. Do not provide them with a grade or feedback on the example assessment; instead, have them individually, in pairs, or in groups (you can give them the option) mark it using the actual marking criteria and provide feedback reflecting the grade they assign. This process supports their understanding of the assessment requirements, how marks are allocated, and what a good assessment should look like before they undertake it for themselves.

Devote Some Class Time to Assessment Work

I've always found that a good way to engage learners and support their interest in and confidence with assessment is to give them some time in class to work on their summative assessments. This approach not only is central to learner motivation (Wormald et al., 2009) but also enables them to benefit from teacher and peer support and ongoing feedback, and to embed important learning points from that day's session directly into their assessments, with opportunities for any clarification. Whenever I've done this in the past, I've made two key observations: class attendance is higher and fewer learners require an extension to their submission deadline—both outcomes that benefit learners, teachers, and the institution.

 PAUSE AND THINK

- The next time you plan a teaching session, how will you incorporate the guidance in this chapter?

11

Diagnostic Assessment

Learner variability represents all of the things that make learners different from each other. As discussed previously, a potentially important source of learner variability among learners is their level of prior knowledge, understanding, and experience with the topic they are about to learn. Each learner has a different starting point for their learning, and therefore the "distance" learners must travel to accomplish the learning goal within the timeframes set out by the curriculum will likely vary quite widely. For this reason, it can be useful to diagnostically assess what learners know (or don't) at the start of a period of instruction as part of your intentional strategy to personalize learning by meeting learners where they are right now.

Differentiated Instruction

Formative, diagnostic assessment, as noted in Chapter 5, is interpreting data on student learning in order to adapt instruction to individual learner needs, and as such is perhaps the single most influential tool teachers have to support effective learning in every learner (Black & William,

1998; Connell, 2020). Connell (2020) argues that one-to-one instruction, in which learning is highly personalized, is the most powerful means of supporting learning, citing Bloom's (1984) work demonstrating that the average learner can accelerate their learning to within 2% of the top-performing learners taught through various group instructional methods. The key problem, however, according to Connell, is that the personalization that is so critical to the success of one-to-one instruction is lost during group instruction. Connell argues that formative assessment is the key way to bridge that gap between one-to-one and group instruction.

To Connell (2020), a critical role of the teacher is to narrow the gap between the curriculum as it actually exists and the curriculum experienced by individual, variable learners. For example, if the gap is too wide and the learner struggles with the learning, it is up to the teacher to find ways to minimize that struggle. If the gap is too narrow and poses no challenge for the learner, it is up to the teacher to find ways to make it more challenging to avoid boredom and disengagement (Connell, 2020). This is essentially differentiated, or targeted, instruction: tailoring instruction and feedback to meet individual learning needs as a means of supporting learners to learn effectively.

Generally, teachers may differentiate content, teaching approaches, the learning environment (and its associated resources and materials), and possibly assessments themselves. Additionally, learners may be differentiated on interests, approaches to learning, and capabilities homogenously (placing learners with similar capabilities together), heterogeneously (placing learners with mixed capabilities together), or even randomly (Wu, 2013).

Let's consider a basic example. A teacher may group learners based on their understanding of a topic by differentiating content. For instance, the teacher may set learning activities that span the various levels of Bloom's taxonomy (Anderson & Krathwohl, 2001; Bloom et al., 1956), with learners who have limited prior understanding of the topic undertaking activities reflecting the lower levels of the taxonomy, supporting their development of the fundamental concepts and ideas related to the topic. Conversely, learners with prior understanding of the topic might be asked to undertake activities that reflect some of the higher levels of the taxonomy. Critically, the content, tasks, and activities the learners are presented with, and the feedback they receive, reflect a particular grouping based on their prior knowledge and understanding. Grouping is flexible, and learners can move between groups as their knowledge and understanding changes. This is just a basic example, but it serves to illustrate the point.

According to McGlynn and Kelly (2017), formative assessment often gives rise to three broad groups of learners:

- Learners who have fully mastered the content and/or skills to be learned and require additional stretch and challenge.
- Learners who have a basic understanding of the content and/or skills to be learned but require some additional support to gain mastery.
- Learners who have no understanding of the content and/or skills to be learned and require extensive support to gain mastery.

To bring everyone up to the same level, which is reflected in all learners meeting the goals of a given learning experience, learners in the latter two groups require targeted (differentiated) instruction to accelerate their learning.

One of the most persuasive theories on learning is constructivism, the idea that we construct our understanding of any given topic, idea, or concept based on what we already know about it, reflecting Ausubel's (1978) declaration that the most important factor influencing learning is what the learner already knows. However, constructive learning is frequently a long, slow, error-strewn, messy, and drawn-out process that is highly individual and not at all visible to a teacher. As a result, it can be difficult to know where learners are with their learning and what support they might need. Therefore, it is essential that we diagnostically monitor learning in an ongoing fashion using formative assessment; in fact, some education scholars, like Connell (2020), argue that formative assessment is the core characteristic of student-centered teaching. Evidence shows that when learners get well-timed feedback on how successfully their learning is progressing, their engagement improves, and they are more motivated to proactively improve their learning (Cohen et al., 2011).

Connell's (2020) model for the application of formative diagnostic assessment, which he calls MEDI (Measure, Evaluate, Diagnose, Intervene), is summarized in Table 6.

Teachers who intentionally and continually evaluate their learners using formative assessment as part of their instructional practices, and who subsequently adapt their instructional approaches, are rarely surprised at learner summative assessment performance (Meyer et al., 2014). In this sense, then, formative assessment reflects the UDL assessment principle that assessment measures both process and product (Meyer et al., 2014).

Table 6: The MEDI Approach to Applying Formative Assessment (Connell, 2020)

Measure	Complete a measurement of learner performance in a formative diagnostic assessment.
Evaluate	Interpret learner performance in the formative diagnostic assessment to gauge their current level of understanding.
Diagnose	Where are the gaps in learning for the learner? What important aspects do they need to improve?
Intervene	Adapt instruction to support the learner to bridge gaps in learning.

UDL and Differentiated Instruction

I often am asked if UDL is just a sophisticated form of differentiation, and my answer is always no. It is true that they have similarities: Both approaches address the failure of traditional education to meet the needs of all learners, for example (Novak, 2022). As Tomlinson and McTighe describe so eloquently in their great book *Integrating Differentiated Instruction and Understanding by Design* (2006), it has become increasingly challenging for teachers to ignore differences in culture, race, gender, experience, disability, personal interest, and learning preferences (to name but a few areas) among modern learners. We've reached a tipping point where we must cater to these wide and varied learning needs and make differentiated instruction a critical part of our instructional planning (Tomlinson & McTighe, 2006).

Despite their similarities, differentiated instruction and UDL differ along some important lines. Differentiation largely represents targeted instruction and is primarily led by the teacher, since it is the teacher who makes the decisions about what the learner needs. Differentiation alone does not enable learners to articulate their own learning goals and strategies, or choose the approaches and tools they require to meet their needs (Novak, 2022). With UDL, on the other hand, learners are the ones making the choices about what they need to be successful with their learning and, in so doing, they develop their self-regulation and executive functioning skills. Hence, UDL could be considered "self-differentiation" (Novak, 2022).

These differences notwithstanding, differentiated instruction and UDL can work together; namely, UDL can be supplemented with differentiated instruction. The "baseline" approach should always be UDL—offering multiple means of engagement, representation, and action and expression from the outset. However, there may be times when targeted instruction is required to accelerate learning. Diagnostic assessment, of course, is necessary to ascertain which learners require targeted instruction. Once groupings are formed, learners should still be offered options and choices as part of a continued commitment to UDL.

PAUSE AND THINK

- Do you use formative diagnostic assessment? If not, why not? Can you start using it?

12

Assessment for Metacognitive Development

The UDL Guidelines contain several important subguidelines reflecting metacognitive skills that are essential to successful learning. This chapter will discuss how the development of those skills is related to assessment processes.

What Is Metacognition?

Metacognition is essentially the process of thinking about one's own thinking and learning. It plays a critical role in "learning to learn" because it involves recognizing when you've achieved understanding of a given topic or concept and when you haven't, as well as knowing what to do in the latter case. For example, you engage in metacognitive processes when you notice that a particular learning strategy isn't working and must be replaced with an alternative one. Additionally, metacognition involves understanding yourself as a learner, including the things you do well from a learning perspective and the things you do less well. Metacognition is an essential lifelong learning skill and represents the second key characteristic of the "expert learner": having personal awareness of how to master learning, as discussed in Chapter 3. Formative assessment approaches, including assessment as learning, are important in helping learners develop their metacognitive capabilities (Nicol & Macfarlane-Dick, 2006).

Sustaining Effort and Persistence

Learning can be challenging, especially when it proceeds slowly or is difficult. Knowing what to do to sustain effort and persistence in the face of learning challenges is a critical metacognitive skill. Various assessment-related learning and teaching endeavors can support development of these skills.

Achievement of learning goals at unit/module level is generally measured via summative assessment. I've discussed the importance of ensuring that assessments represent a clear measure of the learning experience goals—remember, we can't hit a target we can't clearly see. It is equally important to familiarize learners with the learning goals and frequently remind them, in multiple formats, how those goals relate to the assessment. It's imperative to support learners in breaking assessment tasks down into short-term objectives, using various scaffolds and prompts as well as clear examples of what constitutes the desired outcomes. An easy way to do this is to bring assessment into the classroom, as discussed in Chapter 10. For example, using assessment for and as learning strategies can provide the mastery-oriented feedback that supports learners to set short-term assessment objectives, as well as feedback on process-based markers (such as level of effort and improvement). Familiarizing learners with assessment will keep focus on the learning goals and their relationship to the assessment, and "flip the feedback"–type tasks will help learners understand what is required of them, as well as what "good" looks like. Dedicating some class time to assessment completion enables learners to enact their short-term assessment objectives in a supportive environment.

Self-Regulation

Learning is an inherently emotional activity. We've all felt strong (positive and negative) feelings when engaged in a learning experience. *Self-regulation*, sometimes called *emotional self-regulation*, is the ability to regulate one's emotional responses to learning. Again, various assessment-related learning and teaching endeavors can support learners to develop their self-regulation skills.

The first step for any teacher is to clearly recognize and acknowledge that due to its high-stakes nature, assessment is likely to arouse strong feelings in learners. The potential consequences of performing poorly in summative assessments may produce anxiety, trepidation, and dread or fear. This is why self-regulation skills, specifically those associated with assessment completion, are so important.

Many of the aforementioned approaches to sustaining effort and persistence will also support the development of more effective self-regulation. For example, breaking assessment goals down into manageable, short-term personal objectives can support learners to take greater ownership of their assessment and help them develop confidence as they satisfy short-term objectives.

Chapter 7 discussed emotional assessment barriers and provided some EI skills training strategies that could support learners to cope with their emotions and develop their emotional literacy (Brackett & Katulak, 2007). These skills center on recognizing emotions and their intensity, becoming aware of one's current coping strategies and their effectiveness while devising possible alternative strategies, and using emotions to elicit the desired emotional states for learning. Chapter 7 also included some templates to use with learners to facilitate personal coping skills and strategies around assessment.

Assessment as learning strategies that allow learners to self-assess and reflect on their learning have been discussed extensively in this book. Intentional assessment as learning activities present an ideal opportunity to implement some EI skills training. It could even be useful to engage learners in some EI skills training activities in class right after the summative assessment has been presented, discussed, and clarified. How—and how strongly—do they feel about it? How will they regulate their emotions, what else could they do, what emotional state will they need to be in to successfully complete their assessment, and how will they get there?

Executive Function

Executive function broadly refers to a set of skills related to the ability to plan, organize, prioritize, manage, monitor, strategize, control impulses and emotions, think flexibly, and follow direction in the pursuit of goals. It should come as no surprise that executive function skills are essential to successful learning—and particularly successful assessment—outcomes. We must support learners to develop such skills for all learning scenarios, but especially for assessment-related learning.

Ensuring that learners are breaking assessment goals down into manageable, short-term personal objectives, as described previously, can be a useful starting point for developing the executive functioning necessary for successful assessment outcomes. It is important that learners make a habit out of working backward from an assessment submission deadline, determining the short-term milestones they need to achieve as they progress toward satisfying the overarching goal. As a teacher, you should encourage this practice but also support it with examples, prompts, resources, reminders, and scaffolds. Remember, however, that your learners must set their own objectives—you can't do it for them.

Learners must be supported with action planning and strategy development if they are to develop their executive functioning skills. This may include prompting learners to "stop and think" about how they can strategically use a key learning point within their assessment. It may also include providing them with various tools and templates for action planning, prioritization, and sequencing, encouraging and supporting them to "project manage" their assessment to completion by breaking the assessment down into manageable, bite-size "chunks" of short-term objectives, as mentioned previously. Providing models and exemplars here is essential, especially if this approach is new to the learners. Table 7 shows how to break down an assessment task like a research project or dissertation into smaller chunks, with each assigned a specific period to be worked on. The approach used is called a GANTT chart, a visual project management tool that displays tasks along a timeline, showing start and end dates and progress. The chart is named after American engineer and management consultant Henry L. Gantt, who developed the chart in the early 20th century.

Table 7: A Basic GANTT Chart

MONTH	1	2	3	4	5	6
Activity						
Proposal						
Ethical approval						
Intro						
Lit review						
Methods						
Data collection						
Results						
Discussion						

Successful assessment outcomes often rely on the ability to connect new learning to prior knowledge, select and recognize important and irrelevant information, identify key ideas and related concepts, make inferences, and develop strategies to solve problems (Dexter & Hughes, 2011). However, learners may require some support in developing such capabilities, so it is important to provide them with various tools that can help them manage and use information and resources. For example, checklists, graphic organizers, and various organizing and categorizing templates can help learners gather and sort their ideas and information, enabling them to comprehend relationships between concepts and facts more clearly.

Perhaps the final critical executive functioning skill learners require for successful assessment outcomes is the ability to evaluate their own progress toward assessment goals. In order to do this, they require feedback that shows the progress they are (or are not) making. We've discussed the need to bring assessment into class, specifically how we can use assessment briefs, marking criteria, and exemplar work as instructional tools. These tools can also be used as prompts for self-monitoring and reflection. Learners can be prompted to reflect on their progress toward short-term assessment objectives, and may even use some of the aforementioned tools and templates to monitor their progress. A BRAG-rated assessment GANTT chart (see Table 8)—which breaks down an assessment into individual tasks with deadlines and milestones, and where progress against each task is rated as Blue (action completed; represented here as the darkest gray), Red (no progress; shown here as medium gray), Amber (partial progress; shown as the lightest gray), or Green (good progress; not shown in the table)—is a highly visual indicator of progress that can support task planning and prioritization. The dashed vertical line on the chart represents the present time in the process.

Table 8: A BRAG-Rated GANTT Chart

MONTH	1	2	3	4	5	6
Activity						
Proposal	▓					
Ethical approval	▓					
Intro		▓				
Lit review		▓				
Methods				░		
Data collection				░		
Results						░
Discussion						

> **PAUSE AND THINK**
>
> ▫ Do your assessment processes and practices support your learners' metacognitive development?

13

Cheat-Proof Assessment

Academic misconduct is a growing problem in many higher education contexts globally. In its broadest sense, *academic misconduct* refers to any action that attempts to gain, or assists others in gaining, an unfair academic advantage. Some common types of academic misconduct are listed in Table 9. (Please note that this is not an exhaustive list.)

Table 9: Common Types of Academic Misconduct

Plagiarism	Passing off someone else's work as your own
Cheating	Using unauthorized sources/devices to complete your work and passing it off as your own
Contract Cheating	Paying someone to complete your work and passing it off as your own
Collusion	Working together with others to gain an unfair advantage
Fabrication, falsification, or misrepresentation	Providing false information or misrepresenting information or data
Facilitation	Helping others to gain an unfair advantage

A recent concern among higher education institutions has been the rise of generative artificial intelligence (AI) technologies, such as the language processing chatbot ChatGPT, and the potential for learners to submit assessed work authored by such tools, passing it off as their own—a clear example of academic misconduct. There is insufficient scope in this book to explore how assessment design and assessment-related learning might attenuate specific types of academic misconduct. Clearly, different types may require different methods of eradication. The approach in this chapter is more general, focusing more on how we might reduce learner temptation to engage in academic misconduct by creating a learning environment conducive to supporting positive assessment outcomes.

The Context of Cheating

It is difficult to estimate how many learners engage in academic misconduct, but there is evidence to suggest that it is a widespread practice among higher education learners. For example, research by Newton (2018) estimates that one in seven graduates has engaged in *contract cheating* (when a learner hires a third party, such as an essay-writing company or freelance writer, to complete their assessment for them and then submits it as their own), which potentially represents more than 30 million learners across the world. Of course, contract cheating is just one form of academic misconduct, so the actual level in higher education is likely much higher. Academic misconduct occurs across all disciplines and subjects, and across the full range of assessment types. Thus, it is a clear threat to the accountability purpose of assessment presented in Chapter 1, which is the responsibility of educational institutions to the public and/or government to provide evidence that learning is being promoted and subsequent academic standards are being upheld (Archer, 2017).

In reality, phrases like *cheat-proof assessment* aren't helpful because they imply that academic misconduct can be "designed out" of assessment when the reality is that it is unlikely that any kind of cheating can ever be fully eradicated from assessment. Despite this, assessment design remains an important channel to combat academic misconduct, focusing on ways to reduce the opportunity and temptation to engage in academic misconduct (QAA, 2022). Note, however, that our primary focus is on supporting effective learning and subsequent positive assessment outcomes. Reducing opportunity and temptation to engage in academic misconduct is a by-product of this process, not the objective in itself.

Reasons for Academic Misconduct

Academic misconduct occurs for a variety of reasons, with research indicating that learners may engage in it because they see an opportunity to; because they feel dissatisfied with the teaching and learning environment; because they have poor research, attribution, and writing skills; because they feel unable to access learning support; because they lack confidence; because their first language is not English; because they have little interest or capability in the subject of study; because they lack engagement; because they have poor time management skills; or because they don't understand an assessment's requirements (Brimble, 2016; Newton, 2015).

Many of these reasons represent sources of learner variability. Others represent clear barriers to learning. UDL considers learner variability in instructional and curriculum design and works to remove or reduce barriers that arise from the interaction with the sources of learner variability and the learning environment. Hence, one could argue that taking a UDL approach to curriculum design already reduces the probability of academic misconduct by proactively addressing many of the reasons learners cheat.

Integrating Assessment Into Instruction

Perhaps the overarching message of this book is that assessment must become a more intentional and integrated part of instruction if we are to genuinely support learners to demonstrate their learning effectively. This central message also addresses questions around avoiding academic misconduct. There is a much greater likelihood that learners will avoid academic misconduct if we make assessment a more integrated part of their instructional experience, because by doing so, we remove or reduce critical barriers that prevent them from demonstrating their learning effectively. Bringing assessment into the classroom (discussed in Chapter 10) is an important strategy when it comes to avoiding academic misconduct, since assessments completed in a learner's own time (especially written ones), despite being a very well-established mode of assessment, may have the highest risk of academic misconduct (QAA, 2022).

Making Assumptions of Learners

Firstly, one of the critical mistakes we make when assessing learners is assuming they are familiar with and understand the conventions, traditions, and terminology associated with assessment and also possess the skills required to successfully complete assessments. Given the diversity of learners in higher education classrooms today and their variable prior learning experiences, one thing we can safely assume is that many of them won't be familiar with the what, why, and how of assessment. Therefore, we must give learners time and guidance with assessment. For those who are new to higher education, assessment demands are likely more challenging than what they've faced previously.

Preparing learners intentionally for assessment is a must, and the best place for this to happen is in the classroom as part of instruction. This preparation must be timely—for example, there is little point in discussing the assessment requirements only in the first week of teaching, when submission is 12 weeks away! Learners remember what they see, hear, and experience frequently and recently, so we should provide ongoing assessment-related instruction right up to the point of submission.

Critically, assessment-related instruction (teaching and resources or materials) should include supporting learners in developing the knowledge and skills they are required to demonstrate in the assessment itself. For example, learners require support in developing expressive capabilities aligned to the assessment methods (writing, speaking, presenting, etc.) as well as in their ability to find, evaluate, organize, use, and cite the information and academic sources required for assessment. Learners should also be supported to develop their own proofreading and plagiarism-checking capabilities so that they can check their own and others' work.

Assessment-related resources and materials—such as assessment briefs, background information, and instructions—should be presented in multiple formats, in plain English, and with language establishing what learners can do as part of their assessment as opposed to what they should not do, emphasizing academic integrity in a positive way (QAA, 2022).

It's also important to provide assessment-related resources and materials in multiple languages, since language barriers may make it more challenging for learners to demonstrate learning through assessment, especially if language skills are required as part of the assessment process. There is some evidence to suggest that learners studying in another language are more likely to cheat (Bretag et al., 2019), so we must consider the assessment support we give to learners from diverse cultural backgrounds. We can't assume that their previous learning experiences will align directly with the traditions, conventions, and terminology of assessment as we know them, nor can we assume that such learners possess the skills required to successfully complete assessment tasks. Culturally diverse students, especially those for whom English is not a native language, will require support, guidance, and time to achieve successful assessment outcomes. Inflexible or clustered assessment submission deadlines should be avoided for all learners, but especially for those who may require additional time to understand the assessment processes. Teachers concerned about the potential for extra work in this regard should consider using peer-assisted learning approaches.

The Power of Formative Assessment

As noted previously, formative assessment is the most important form of assessment from a UDL perspective. It may also play an integral role in reducing incidences of academic misconduct. Formative assessment is low stakes and so affords learners the opportunity to develop the knowledge, skills, and competencies required for summative assessment. Critically, it enables teachers to better understand where learners are, enabling them to adapt their instruction and further personalize learning, which in itself may reduce the temptation to cheat. It is also a fabulous mechanism for teachers to get familiar with learner work, including idiosyncrasies of expressive style, knowledge, attitudes, and confidence. This presents two huge advantages: it is easier for teachers to spot academic misconduct if they're familiar with individual learner work, and learners are perhaps less likely to cheat if they know their teachers are familiar with their work. Indeed, there is some indication that learners may be more likely to commit academic misconduct if their teachers do not know their work well (Bretag et al., 2019).

Formative assessment can be used as a summative assessment "checkpoint," or a gauge of where learners are in terms of the requirements of summative assessment. Teachers can indicate learners' progress toward summative assessment goals using medal and mission feedback (Petty, 2014), introduced in Chapter 4, and by setting bespoke goals and signposting further outlets for support, such as extracurricular study support services. Goal setting against the requirements of a summative assessment can't really happen without a formative assessment. Indeed, a formative assessment could be a draft(s) of the summative assessment task undertaken in a timely fashion ahead of submission.

As discussed in Chapter 12, it could be useful for learners to keep assessment planners or a GANTT chart to track their progress toward summative assessment completion, including formative assessment outcomes.

Authenticity and Occupational Relevance

Authentic or occupationally relevant assessments provide a realistic preview of situations learners may experience in the workplace, requiring them to use knowledge and skills in ways relevant to occupational or employment contexts. These assessments may include (but aren't limited to) practical assessments; assessments on placements; and context-specific, personalized, and peer-based approaches. They may also make it more difficult to engage in various forms of academic misconduct, such as contract cheating (QAA, 2022). Chapter 8 explored some key differences between primarily assessing skills and competencies versus primarily assessing knowledge. One key benefit of primarily assessing skills and competencies is that authenticity and occupational relevance are usually built in. As noted in that chapter, the most valid and relevant way to assess a public speaking course would be through some sort of public speaking task, a highly authentic assessment for this context and one that would be difficult to cheat on.

As also mentioned in Chapter 8, when learners are asked to demonstrate their knowledge—factual, conceptual, procedural, or metacognitive—of a topic or concept as part of an assessment, they are frequently required to demonstrate their knowledge in a written form (an essay, report, literature review, etc.). It's crucial to consider whether such written outputs are the most authentic and occupationally relevant means to demonstrate learning. It may be more valid to focus on what a learner can do in relation to their learning rather than what they can write about. Furthermore, providing a range of authentic and relevant assessment types as per vocational qualifications may disincentivize learners from engaging in forms of academic misconduct (QAA, 2022).

PAUSE AND THINK

- What forms of academic misconduct are a problem in your context? What advice in this chapter will you use to combat academic misconduct?

Epilogue

If you take just one idea from this book, let it be this: Assessment must become an intentional part of instruction if it is to effectively support learning and if learners are to perform well in assessment tasks. When we think about assessment as part of the broader process of learning, rather than as just the means of demonstrating learning, we are better able to tap into its huge potential to develop expert learning capability among all learners.

Furthermore, when we think about the accessibility, inclusivity, and equitability of our assessment designs by incorporating Universal Design for Learning principles, we can be confident we are taking the first critical steps toward making assessment learnable, preserving critical learner cognitive resources, and intentionally reducing or removing the barriers that often prevent learners from clearly and effectively demonstrating what they know or can do, which can be the most liberating of learning experiences. Remember the saying from Chapter 3: "Everyone is a genius, but if you judge a fish by its ability to climb a tree, it will live its whole life believing that it is stupid." Imagine, then, how that fish would feel if it were judged by its ability to swim. Its perception and view of itself and its capabilities would be radically transformed for the better, and this is what learning is about: positive transformation. The process of assessment plays a huge role in transformation but not always in a positive way, and we have the capacity to change this.

Finally, as part of intentionally bringing assessment into the classroom, don't forget the powerful role assessment plays in personalizing and targeting instruction, as well as in catalyzing adaptations to our teaching approaches. In the effective classroom, everything is done by design, including when, where, and how assessment is used to further develop instruction and the broader curricula. Enjoy your assessment journey!

References and Further Reading

Anderson, L. W., & Krathwohl, D. R. (Eds.). (2001). *A taxonomy for learning, teaching, and assessing: A revision of Bloom's Taxonomy of educational objectives*. Allyn & Bacon.

Archer, E. (2017, August). The assessment purpose triangle: Balancing the purposes of educational assessment. *Frontiers in Education, 2*(41). https://doi.org/10.3389/feduc.2017.00041

Ausubel, D. (1978). *Educational psychology: A cognitive view*. Holt.

Black, P., Harrison, C., Hodgen, J., Marshall, B., & Serret, N. (2010). Validity in teachers' summative assessments. *Assessment in Education: Principles, Policy & Practice, 17*(2), 215–232. https://doi.org/10.1080/09695941003696016

Black, P., & Wiliam, D. (1998). Assessment and classroom learning. *Assessment in Education: Principles, Policy & Practice, 5*(1), 7–74. https://doi.org/10.1080/0969595980050102

Bloom, B. S. (1984). The 2 Sigma problem: The search for methods of group instruction as effective as one-to-one tutoring. *Educational Researcher, 13*(6), 4–16. https://www.jstor.org/stable/1175554

Bloom, B. S., Engelhart, M. D., Furst, E. J., Hill, W. H., & Krathwohl, D. R. (1956). *Handbook I: Cognitive domain*. David McKay.

Brackett, M. A., & Katulak, N. A. (2007). Emotional intelligence in the classroom: Skill-based training for teachers and students. In J. Ciarrochi & J. D. Mayer (Eds.), *Applying emotional intelligence: A practitioner's guide* (pp. 1–27). Psychology Press.

Bretag, T., Harper, R., Burton, M., Ellis, C., Newton, P., Rozenberg, P., Saddiqui, S., & van Haeringen, K. (2019). Contract cheating: A survey of Australian university students. *Studies in Higher Education*, 44(11), 1837–56. https://doi.org/10.1080/03075079.2018.1462788

Brimble, M. (2016). Why students cheat: An exploration of the motivators of student academic dishonesty in higher education. In T. Bretag (Ed.), *Handbook of academic integrity* (pp. 365–82). Springer Singapore.

Carless, D., Salter, D., Yang, M., & Lam, J. (2011). Developing sustainable feedback practices. *Studies in Higher Education*, 36(4), 395–407. https://doi.org/10.1080/03075071003642449

Cohen, N., Hall, T., Vue, G., & Ganley, P. (2011). The strategic reader: Using curriculum-based measurement and universal design for learning to support reading instruction in a digital environment. In P. E. Noyce & D. T. Hickey (Eds.), *New frontiers in formative assessment* (pp. 72–83). Harvard Education Press.

Connell, M. W. (2020). *Using formative assessment to improve student outcomes in classrooms.* CAST Professional Publishing.

Dexter, D. D., & Hughes, C. A. (2011). Graphic organizers and students with learning disabilities: A meta-analysis. *Learning Disability Quarterly*, 34(1), 51–72. https://doi.org/10.1177/073194871103400104

Earl, L. M, & Katz, S. (2006). *Rethinking classroom assessment with purpose in mind: Assessment for learning, assessment as learning, and assessment of learning.* Manitoba Education, Citizenship and Youth. https://www.edu.gov.mb.ca/k12/assess/wncp/full_doc.pdf

Evans, C. (2013). Making sense of assessment feedback in higher education. *Review of Educational Research, 83*(1), 70–120. https://doi.org/10.3102/0034654312474350

Gardner, J. (Ed.). (2011). *Assessment and learning* (2nd ed.). SAGE Publications Ltd.

Griffiths, C. M., Murdock-Perriera, L., & Eberhardt, J. L. (2023). "Can you tell me more about this?": Agentic written feedback, teacher expectations, and student learning. *Contemporary Educational Psychology, 73,* 102145. https://doi.org/10.1016/j.cedpsych.2022.102145

Hall, T. E., Meyer, A., & Rose, D. H. (Eds.). (2012). *Universal design for learning in the classroom: Practical applications.* Guilford Press.

Kibble, J. D. (2017). Best practices in summative assessment. *Advances in Physiology Education, 41*(1), 110–19. https://doi.org/10.1152/advan.00116.2016

Lysaght, Z., & O'Leary, M. (2013). An instrument to audit teachers' use of assessment for learning. *Irish Educational Studies, 32*(2), 217–32. https://doi.org/10.1080/03323315.2013.784636

McGlynn, K., & Kelly, J. (2017). Using formative assessments to differentiate instruction. *Science Scope, 41*(4), 22–25. https://doi.org/10.2505/4/ss17_041_04_22

Merry, K. L. (2023). *Delivering inclusive and impactful instruction: Universal Design for Learning in higher education.* CAST Professional Publishing.

Meyer, A., Rose, D. H., & Gordon, D. (2014). *Universal design for learning: Theory and Practice.* CAST Professional Publishing.

Morales-Martinez, G. E., Trejo-Quintana, J., Charles-Cavazos, D. J., Mezquita-Hoyos, Y. N., & Sanchez-Monroy, M. (2021). Chronometric constructive cognitive learning evaluation model: Measuring the construction of the human cognition schema of psychology students. *International Journal of Learning, Teaching and Educational Research, 20*(2), 1–21. https://dx.doi.org/10.26803/ijlter.20.5.4

Newton, P. (2015). Academic integrity: A quantitative study of confidence and understanding in students at the start of their higher education. *Assessment and Evaluation in Higher Education*, *41*(3), 482–97. https://doi.org/10.1080/02602938.2015.1024199

Newton, P. M. (2018, August). How common is commercial contract cheating in higher education and is it increasing? A systematic review. *Frontiers in Education*, *3*(67). https://doi.org/10.3389/feduc.2018.00067

Nicol, D. J., & Macfarlane-Dick, D. (2006). Formative assessment and self-regulated learning: A model and seven principles of good feedback practice. *Studies in Higher Education*, *31*(2), 199–218. https://doi.org/10.1080/03075070600572090

Novak, K. (2022). *UDL now! A teacher's guide to applying Universal Design for Learning*. CAST Professional Publishing.

Petty, G. (2014). *Teaching today: A practical guide*. Oxford University Press.

Phelps, R. P. (2005). *Defending standardized testing*. Psychology Press.

Posey, A., & Bastoni, A. (2021). *The assessment playbook: A UDL approach*. CAST Professional Publishing.

Quality Assurance Agency. (2022). *Contracting to cheat in higher education: How to address essay mills and contract cheating*. The Quality Assurance Agency for Higher Education.

Race, P. (2019). *The lecturer's toolkit: A practical guide to assessment, learning and teaching*. Routledge.

Rose, D. H., Hall, T. E., & Murray, E. (2008). Accurate for all: Universal Design for Learning and the assessment of students with learning disabilities. *Perspectives on Language and Literacy*, *34*(4), 23–28.

Rose, D. H., & Meyer, A. (2002). *Teaching every student in the digital age: Universal Design for Learning*. Association for Supervision and Curriculum Development (ASCD).

Rose, D. H., Robinson, K. H., Hall, T. E., Coyne, P., Jackson, R. M., Stahl, W. M., & Wilcauskas, S. L. (2018). Accurate and informative for all: Universal Design for Learning (UDL) and the future of assessment. In S. Elliott, R. Kettler, P. Beddow, & A. Kurz (Eds.), *Handbook of accessible instruction and testing practices: Issues, innovations, and applications* (pp. 167–180). Springer.

Rowntree, D. (2015). *Assessing students: How shall we know them?* Routledge.

Sadler, D. R. (1989). Formative assessment and the design of instructional systems. *Assessment in Education, 5*(1), 77–84.

Sadler, D. R. (2009). Transforming holistic assessment and grading into a vehicle for complex learning. In G. Joughin (Ed.), *Assessment, learning and judgement in higher education* (pp. 1–19). Springer.

Sadler, D. R. (2010). Beyond feedback: Developing student capability in complex appraisal. *Assessment and Evaluation in Higher Education, 35*(5), 535–50.

Salvia, J., Ysseldyke, J., & Witmer, S. (2009). *Assessment in special and inclusive education* (11th ed.). Houghton Mifflin.

Supovitz, J. (2010). *Is high-stakes testing working?* University of Pennsylvania Graduate School of Education.

Sweller, J., van Merriënboer, J. J., & Paas, F. (1998). Cognitive architecture and instructional design. *Educational Psychology Review, 10*, 251–296. https://doi.org/10.1007/s10648-019-09465-5

Sweller, J., van Merriënboer, J. J., & Paas, F. (2019). Cognitive architecture and instructional design: 20 years later. *Educational Psychology Review, 31*, 261–292. https://doi.org/10.1007/s10648-019-09465-5

Tomlinson, C. A., and McTighe, J. (2006). *Integrating differentiated instruction and understanding by design*. Association for Supervision and Curriculum Development (ASCD).

Wiggins, G., & McTighe, J. (2005). *Understanding by design.* Association for Supervision and Curriculum Development (ASCD).

Wormald, B. W., Schoeman, S., Somasunderam, A., & Penn, M. (2009). Assessment drives learning: An unavoidable truth? *Anatomical Sciences Education, 2*(5), 199–204. https://doi.org/10.1002/ase.102

Wu, E. W. (2013). The path to differentiation: An interview with Carol Tomlinson. *Journal of Advanced Academics, 24*(2), 125–33. https://doi.org/10.1177/1932202X13483472

CAST Skinny Books®

"Don't tell me everything. Just give me the skinny!"™

CAST Professional Publishing produces books that help educators at all levels improve their practice—and change students' lives—through Universal Design for Learning (UDL). We create, nurture, and distribute exceptional media products that inspire and inform educational research, instructional practice, and policy making for the betterment of all.

Skinny Books by CAST address critical topics of education practice through brief, informative publications that emphasize practical tips and strategies. We talk about these books as "multivitamins"—densely packed with helpful knowledge in a small, digestible format.

We welcome new proposals. Got an idea? Let us know at *publishing@cast.org*.

While every Skinny Book will be in tune with the inclusive principles of Universal Design for Learning, not every title needs to address UDL specifically. For those that do, the authors may assume readers have a knowledge of UDL already, as we've done in *Art for All*.

If you need an introduction to UDL, visit *udlguidelines.cast.org*.

You can also purchase this or many other titles on UDL from *www.castpublishing.org*.

MORE FROM CAST

CAST is a nonprofit education research and development organization that created the Universal Design for Learning framework and UDL Guidelines. Our mission is to transform education design and practice until learning has no limits.

CAST supports learners and educators at every level through a variety of offerings:

- Innovative professional development
- Accessibility and inclusive technology resources
- Research, design, and development of inclusive and effective solutions
- Credentials for Universal Design for Learning
- And much more

Visit *www.cast.org* to learn more.

www.ingramcontent.com/pod-product-compliance
Lightning Source LLC
Chambersburg PA
CBHW070114080526
44586CB00013B/1294